Contents

The Author

Lieutenant Colonel Amrine is a career space operator with experience in operations, acquisition, staff and in-theater support to combat operations. He is a Joint Specialty Officer and also a member of the Acquisition Corps. Colonel Amrine has served with Air Force Systems Command, National Reconnaissance Office, U.S. Space Command and Air Force Space Command. Colonel Amrine, a native of Hawaii, was commissioned in 1982 from the Air Force Academy. His first assignment was as a spacecraft operations officer at Sunnyvale AFB. In 1986, he was assigned to the Secretary of the Air Force/Special Projects (SAF/SP) as the Chief, Performance Assessment Branch at Onizuka AFB. In 1988, he was assigned to the Pentagon as a Space Systems Program Manger in a Joint Program Office. In 1993, Colonel Amrine was transferred to Los Angeles AFB as the Chief, Mission Management Systems Division in a SAF/SP program office. In 1995, Col. Amrine was assigned to U.S. Space Command as the Chief, Special Operations Branch. In 1997, Colonel Amrine was assigned to RAF Feltwell, UK as the operations officer of the 5th Space Surveillance Squadron and eleven months later became the commander. While a commander, his squadron was #1 in the 21 Space Wing and #2 in all of AFSPC for Space Operations in AFSPC's 1999 Guardian Challenge. In addition, his unit maxed the first-ever, limited ORI in the 10-year history of the unit. Finally, this unit deployed personnel three times to support combat operations in Kosovo and once to OPERATION NORTHERN WATCH. Before coming to Air War College, Colonel Amrine competed for a White House Fellowship and successfully made it to the regional finals. Upon completion of Air War College in residence, Colonel Amrine will be reassigned to the 30th Operations Group located at Vandenberg AFB as the Operations Group Deputy Commander.

Colonel Amrine's secondary education began at the United States Air Force Academy where he graduated in 1982 with a Bachelor's of Science. In 1992, he graduated from the Air Force Institute of Technology with a Master's of Science in Space Operations. Colonel Amrine has attended all of the Air Force's Professional Military Education schools. In 1989, he graduated from Squadron Officer's School as the #1 graduate, a Distinguished Graduate, class president, and outstanding contributor to his section. In 1995, he graduated from Air Command and Staff College as a distinguished graduate. In 1996, he attended the Armed Forces Staff College for Phase II Joint PME and in 1999, he completed AWC by correspondence.

Acknowledgements

First and foremost, I would like to thank the Lord for the opportunity to attend Air War College and write on a subject that is of great importance to the Air Force as well as to me personally. As with any great endeavor, it is rarely the work of a single person but rather the combined, team effort of many people. This paper is no exception; many people helped me to make it what it is. To Dr. Grant Hammond who served as my thesis advisor, thanks for the motivation and endless supply of ideas and resources. You were the catalyst for this paper being written. To Col. Ted Hailes (ret) and Col. (s) Dave Ziegler, thanks for your detailed reviews and edits of my thoughts. You have both made it a better paper than it was. Thanks to Lt. Col. Sam Greaves who served as a sounding board and never tired of listening to my ideas on how to advance space. Many others contributed either by conversation or e-mail: Lt. Col. Bryant Anderson, Mr. Brent Marley, Col. (s) Earl Matthews, and Lt. Col. Kevin McLaughlin. An additional thanks is owed to Mr. Allen Sexton who sent me a continual stream of space articles, many of which ended up in this paper. Finally, I owe a debt of gratitude to my family for putting up with this paper. To Katherine and Mary Beth, thank you for loving giving up many of your nights and weekends so Daddy could write this paper. To my wife, Elizabeth, thanks for all your love and support in another max effort. I could not have done it without your help. You are the *joie de ma vie!*

v

Abstract

This paper develops a compelling case for a national space vision to advance the American vital interests of prosperity and security. The first half of paper focuses on laying the background for the vision that follows in the second half. In the title, prosperity is listed before security since it is the reason for exploration and eventually requires protection.

The paper begins with the premise that space is becoming an information center of gravity that is increasingly important to the commercial sector as well as the military. However, a major stumbling block in this transition is the lack of the means to protect on-orbit space systems. Without this capability, true command of space is not possible. The paper then transitions to a discourse on the current dependence on space in America. Next, the quest for wealth and information by the European powers in the second millennium is discussed. Each of these examples demonstrates a recurring cycle in their quest: knowledge, exploitation, investment, consumption and protection. This same cycle is seen in the early days of space where the focus was almost exclusively on knowledge and exploration. Several who possessed a vision to advance space were Jules Verne, Wernher von Braun and Arthur C. Clark. From the early days of space, the transition is made to reviewing a current space system, Global Positioning System, as an example of the promise of space and the current focus on investment and consumption.

To make the case for protecting space assets, the role of the U.S. Navy in protecting maritime commerce is examined as well as the current threat to the space sector.

The vision for space focuses on the near-term and primarily on the Air Force. While it is recognized that space is much larger, consisting of the military, intelligence, civil and commercial sectors, to thoroughly discuss each sector is beyond the scope of this paper. The Air Force is singled out since it controls nearly ninety percent of the DOD's white-world space budget and contains nearly the same percentage of space personnel. Fundamental changes are recommended in each of these areas: organization, space doctrine, changing the space culture, professional military education, funding/core competencies, and a review of whether to integrate or separate space capabilities. In addition to these, recommendations are also made for the president and Congress to advance toward the goal of commanding space.

The future requires a national effort to master all sectors of space for America to realize its vital interests of prosperity and security. The vision—to command space—is an economic and political imperative, which in turn will require a military capability. It is a matter of quality of life as well as national security.

Chapter 1

The Premise

The Present

Where there is no vision, the people perish.

Proverbs 29:18

Man's flight through life is sustained by the power of his knowledge.

Eagle and Fledglings Monument
U.S. Air Force Academy

"The Command of Space: A National Vision for American Prosperity and Security" is a title that if not explained may be misunderstood. The first word requiring clarification is "command." Typically, when one hears the term, it is associated with a military officer acting as a commander over a unit. This is not the meaning associated with this title. Rather, "command" is used in the following context: power to control or dominate by position or simply "mastery."[1] The next word requiring illumination is "space." The use of space in the title is not confined to military space only but also the civil, intelligence and commercial sectors of space. Thus, "The Command of Space" implies the ability to control or dominate all sectors of space due to the mastery of this medium by a nation.

The Tofflers in their book *War and Anti-War*, develop the theme that "the way we make war, reflects the way we make wealth."[2] How do we make war? DESERT STORM was called the "first space war" as well as the "first information war."[3] While this link between information and space may not have been appreciated at the time, it was certainly so as we approached the new millennium. All the services had begun a transformation to better integrate space and information. By 1999, all documents produced by the Joint Staff or by the services began with either information superiority or information dominance. In addition, *Joint Vision 2010, Army After Next, From the Sea* and *Global Engagement* all place a strong emphasis on the exploitation of space.[4] *Joint Vision 2020* continues the relation between space and information. Early on, information superiority is singled out as the enabler for full spectrum dominance. Later in the document, space operations are emphasized as equally important as information operations.[5] While this is all theoretical, actual combat operations are reflecting this same mindset.

The rise of the information warrior in combat has begun. In Kosovo, the first-ever Info Operations (IO) cell was established to integrate these capabilities into the fight.[6] With their demonstrated success, their value and creditability is also rising. The merger of Air Intelligence Agency, which contains the Air Force's IO warriors, into Air Combat Command (ACC) earlier this year, is proof that the Air Force's warrior community appreciates these new roles and missions. The military values these new types of warriors, wants more of them and is willing to pay for their full four-year education.[7] The reasons are clear. During ALLIED FORCE, Lt. Gen. Cook, reminded the U.S. and British militaries that almost every piece of information used by the U.S. military either comes from or is transmitted through space.[8] Space and the related information flow is the enabler for military supremacy in combat. If this is the way the U.S. presently makes war, how does this country make wealth?

Using the Toffler axiom and reading the way we currently conduct war, the answer would naturally be "We make wealth through the use of space and information." This conclusion does not mean that space and information are the only way we make wealth as a nation but rather it is one that deserves further analysis. It is important to make the distinction at this point, that when the term "wealth" is used, it means more than just dollars, it also includes quality of life. The Tofflers make the case that the U.S. economy already transitioned to a "Third Wave" or information-based economy. They point to 1956, the first year that white-collar and service employees outnumbered blue-collar factory workers.[9] In a Third Wave economy, the central resource is knowledge.[10] More recently, Thomas Friedman discusses the reality of rapidly flowing information in the globalization era that we now live in. Information technologies are allowing nations, companies and individuals to reach farther, faster, cheaper, and deeper around the world that ever before.[11] With the world becoming more and more "connected" each day, the world is becoming a smaller place. With all these trends, information is a dominant factor in the U.S.'s ability to make wealth as a nation. In that so much information originates in or transmits thorough space, the added importance of space, as well as information, is undeniable.

Holding the high ground and knowing more are inextricably linked in military history. These concepts have their origins in land warfare, where military strategists taught that if one held ground higher than your opponent did on the battlefield; your chances of success were increased. This was true in part because one could see further, and hence, know more about the disposition of enemy forces. It was harder to defeat one who held the high ground. Space is called the "ultimate high ground" in military circles. A pertinent question is, "The high ground of what?" The answer is information. Space allows a perspective that is unlike any other. It is a "God's eye" view. With perspective comes the ability to see and therefore to know. With knowing comes knowledge, and knowledge is the leverage this nation employs for a comparative advantage in the global arena.

It is not only in military affairs that this is so. Knowledge, particularly the rapid, near real time global dissemination of information that is about events and activities throughout the globe, is the key to much of scientific progress, successful investment and commercial success. International political economy is about the movement of goods, service, people, ideas and money. All are aided by improved information flows and these are increasingly space dependent. Both a nation's prosperity and security, now and in the future, are thus linked to space.

Center of gravity is an engineering term that was borrowed by the military community. In a military context, a COG is the hub about which all power is centered and rotates. Using this same definition, it can be said that space is a COG for security and prosperity. Much of the nation's wealth and security is founded on space assets and related technology. To understand this concept more thoroughly, the linkage between space and wealth/security is discussed in greater detail in the paper. A better characterization of space is to say space is becoming a COG of information. All of this discussion lays the groundwork for why a vision is needed now.

Most Americans have little understanding of their dependence on space and space-based information flows. Worrying about, let alone investing in space is not a high priority. Life is good and the Cold War is over. But, even though the nation is enjoying its post-Cold War security and prosperity a vision for space is needed. Congress is concerned with this lack of vision. In 2000, three commissions reviewed the space community and its related organizations.[12] Another reason a vision is needed is that the nation is engaged in a different kind of war. It is an economic contest to maintain and expand the wealth of the U.S. Both allies—the European Union (EU)—and current or future adversaries—China—compete with the U.S. China is expected to surpass the size of the U.S. economy in about ten years. While a vision for space may not prevent this, a lack of vision will only hasten American economic and military weakness.

The question is how will this nation secure greater wealth and security in the future? Whatever the specific answer, the increased reliance on space and information are part of the answer. This nation will have to employ the principle of "strategic innovation." This concept calls for fundamentally reinventing the basis of competition in existing markets and inventing entirely new markets.[13] It requires "out of the box" thinking—business as usual will not keep the nation competitive in this new information-based, global economy. Ultimately, the U.S. will have to invest in the protection of the "information pipeline" in space.[14]

The protection of space assets and the related information flows is vital to the nation's future. In a few years, the U.S.'s total investment in space will approach $500 billion while the amount of money invested and returned from space and related industries over the next five years will amount to $2 trillion.[15] While one begins to appreciate the value of space to the nation's well being with these numbers, what many would find shocking is that there exists little to no means to protect this wealth. History shows wealth accumulation will not go uncontested. The nation must prepare now for a future that is secure in space. To command space is a national imperative for American prosperity and security.

Notes

[1] Webster's New World Dictionary, 2nd College Edition, (United States: William Collins + World Publishing Company, Inc., 1978), 284.

[2] Alvin Toffler and Heidi Toffler, *War and Anti-War: Survival at the Dawn of the Twenty-First Century*, (Boston, MA: Little, Brown and Company, 1993), 3.

[3] General Tony McPeak, then Chief of Staff of the Air Force, called DESERT STORM the first space war. A number of other generals, both U.S. and allied wrote a book after the Gulf War entitled *The First Information War*. Alan D. Campen, Contributing Editor, *The First Information War*, (Fairfax, VA: AFCEA International Press, 1992).

[4] General Thomas S. Moorman, Jr., "Integrating Air and Space: Defining the Orbit" January 12, 1999, National Press Club, 18; on-line, Internet, November 28, 2000, available from http://www.aef.org/eak12jan99.html.

[5] Joint Staff, *Joint Vision 2020*, (Washington D.C.: U.S. Government Printing Office, June 2000), 7, 30.

[6] Major General David F. MacGhee, "Emerging Concepts on AF Employment," lecture, Air War College, Maxwell Air Force Base, AL., 7 December 2000.

[7] The 2001 Defense Authorization Act gave the Pentagon $15 million for grant and scholarships for those seeking a degree in information assurance. This field includes such areas as computer security and guarding networks against cyber-attacks. A four-degree would have a three-year commitment. The full scholarship would cover tuition, fees, books, laboratory expenses, and room and board. Vince Crawley, "Stay in, get a full ride, Pentagon to offer full scholarships to recruits with high-tech ambition," *Air Force Times*, November 13, 2000, 20.

[8] Lieutenant General Donald G. Cook, "Royal United Services Institute for Defense Studies Military Utility of Space Conference Keynote Address," Whitehall, London, September 8, 1999, 6; on-line, Internet, November 28, 2000, available from http://www.spacecom.af.mil/hqafspc/library/speeches/royal_inst.htm.

[9] The First and Second Wave economies were characterized as agrarian and industrial respectively. Toffler, 57.

[10] Toffler, 58.

[11] Thomas L. Friedman, *The Lexus and the Olive Tree*, (New York: Anchor Books, 2000), 9.

[12] Three different commissions examined the National Imagery and Mapping Agency (NIMA), the National Reconnaissance Office (NRO), and the Organization and

Notes

Management of DOD Space. All three of these commissions are briefly reviewed in this paper.

[13] Gary Hamel, "The Quest for New Wealth," Spring 1997, 10; on-line, Internet, December 1, 2000, available from http://www.strategosnet.com/articles/quest.html.

[14] Lt. Col. Dave Ziegler, 76 SOPS/CC, Peterson AFB, CO, provided the idea of an "information pipeline" while reviewing a draft of this paper, 12 March 2001.

[15] "Escalating Space Race," 5 January 2001, 3; on-line, Internet, January 8, 2001, available from http://www.stratfor.com/home/giu/archive/010701.asp and Richard J. Newman, "The new space race," U.S. News and World Report, November 8, 1999, 7; on-line, Internet, November 13, 2000, available from http://www.usnews.com/usnews/issue/991108/space.htm and General Howell M. Estes, Commander in Chief, United States Space Command, address to Congressional Committee, Washington D.C., 1998, 17; on-line, Internet, 27 October 2000, available from http://sac.saic.com/space/docs/speeches/speech9.htm.

Chapter 2

Dependence on Space

I would like to register my concern that Americans remain largely ill-informed about their growing dependence on space systems.[16]

General Howell M. Estes III
Commander in Chief,
United States Space Command
Opening remarks in congressional testimony
1998

A Day in the Life of an American

Today, Americans depend on space for critical day-to-day activities, even though most don't recognize the extent. Perhaps the best way to illustrate this dependence is to proceed through the day of an American engineer to see where she interacts with space assets or space-derived technology. Jane is a mechanical-aerospace engineer who designs aircraft components for a European commercial aircraft company. She begins her day by opening the front door and picking up the daily *Wall Street Journal*. After pursuing the *Journal* for 15 minutes, she turns on CNN to catch the latest in world events. While watching CNN, Christiana Amanpour reports live from Europe on the breakdown of trade negotiations between the EU and the United States. After the CNN "Headline News," Jane changes the station to the Weather Channel to receive the current weather forecast. After dressing appropriately for the day, she eats her breakfast and gets ready to depart. On her way out the door, she activates the security system, ensures the fire alarm is working and unplugs her laptop with the NiCd battery fully charged.

During her commute to work, she receives a message on her pager. Her boss asks her to attend a meeting at the customer's new offices. Having never been there, Jane enters the address into her on-board navigation system and reads the directions. Upon arrival, she updates the customer on the project's current status via a video teleconference with the customer's corporate offices in Belgium. After the meeting, Jane departs for her office but stops on the way for gas using the quick-pay pumps by swiping her credit card. At the office she accesses the Internet to locate a particular supplier in Germany. After a successful search, Jane calls the German company and orders the composite materials necessary for the aircraft project. After the call, she notices a high-priority package did not arrive before ten o'clock and so she makes a call to the overnight delivery company to locate the package. While on the phone, the customer service representative accesses the fleet tracking application and informs Jane that the package will be delivered before twelve o'clock. With a break in the action, Jane takes time out to drink a glass of filtered water before getting back on the web. Once on line, she surfs to her local realtor's home page to shop for new homes. Rather than just view static scenes of the house, she is able to view the inside of the house with an interactive 360-degree perspective—a virtual home. Looking at her watch, she notices it is almost time to leave for her medical appointment. With no time for lunch, Jane buys a health food bar wrapped in a silvery Mylar package and a canned juice. After the quick lunch, she deposits the can and wrapper into a manual trash compactor.

At the doctor's office, Jane is subject to the obligatory temperature and blood pressure check. Following this preliminary check, her family doctor performs a mammogram using the latest imaging technology to search for breast cancer. While waiting for the results, the doctor mentions the latest method for taking a biopsy if a suspicious spot is seen—stereotactic biopsy. After the doctor gives a clean bill of health, Jane asks a few medical questions about her parents. With her Dad recently suffering a heart attack, she is concerned and asks about the effectiveness of the laser angioplasty procedure in keeping his arteries clear. Next, she asks the doctor why the medical team installed a programmable pacemaker rather than implanting a miniature defibrillator. With these questions answered, she schedules a follow-on appointment with the receptionist to check if she is prone to osteoporosis. The receptionist mentions the procedure is now much more convenient since X-rays are no longer needed.

Returning back to the office, Jane's boss reminds her that the company's golf tournament is scheduled to start in one hour. Out on the golf course, she reapplies her lipstick that provides UV protection. Being only an average golfer, who still has difficulty judging distances to the pin, she rents a ParView golf cart. This cart accurately tells her the exact distance to the pin on every stroke. After paying for the green fees and cart with her credit card, Jane begins the tournament with her foursome. On hole seven, she receives a cellular phone call from the German company to confirm the receipt of her composites order. While on hole number eleven, the rain begins to sprinkle, and so Jane pulls out her jacket that is insulated with high-tech plastic fibers. She continues to play the course since her personal lightening detection system does not indicate lightening in the area. After scoring a 92 on the course, she stops at the local Home Depot before heading home. Jane's weekend project is to increase her home's energy efficiency so she purchases insulation as well as a radiant barrier to shield the house from the Sun's energy. As she gets into her car, her sunglasses fall to the ground. Jane picks them up and notices the scratch-resistant coating protected her glasses. Upon arrival home, she appreciates the air conditioner thermostat has automatically cooled the house down even though it is 90 degrees outside. As she relaxes in her favorite chair, Jane listens to her latest jazz CD on the surround sound stereo system. With a clear mind, Jane logs on to her computer to check the results of the stock market and places an order with her broker to be executed the next day. After preparing and eating dinner, she departs for her distance learning class in CATIA—leading edge software for computer aided design, manufacturing and engineering. After class, Jane stops at the school's ATM to get some money for tomorrow's lunch. With her money retrieved, Jane gets into her car and turns on the Sirius radio. She enjoys the drive home by listening to CD-quality music with no advertisements. Back at her house, she relishes an old black and white film on the Movie Channel before retiring for the night.

While this day in the life of Jane may not match your typical day, it is significant that she used information from space or was exposed to space technology in over 40 different ways.[17] All of these technologies are available today and our usage of most is routine. Many are so reliable that we use them without ever realizing just how dependent we are becoming on them. We take the use of space and the products we have created to explore it for granted. What is even more noteworthy is that as the information market increasingly drives the American economy, the dependence on space assets will only increase. America's success in the global economy is inextricably linked to exploiting information and the reliance on space as the locus of gathering or transmitting that information. Space and our efforts to explore it, utilize it and command it effect our daily lives to an extraordinary degree.

Notes

[16] General Howell M. Estes, Commander in Chief, United States Space Command, address to Congressional Committee, Washington D.C., 1998, 17; on-line, Internet, 27 October 2000, available from http://sac.saic.com/space/docs/speeches/speech9.htm.

[17] In this chapter, there are 41 uses of the current space infrastructure, space technology or spin off technology from space research. To help the reader in finding each use of space technology, I have called them out individually. 1) Wall Street Journal—National newspapers are typically not created in the home office and then flown around the country to every city that subscribes. Rather, it is increasingly common for the paper to be sent in softcopy via a satellite-communications link (granted it could go via landlines), to a local printer for printing. D. N. Baker et al., "Space Environmental Conditions During April and May 1998: An Indicator for the Upcoming Solar Maximum," 9; on-line, Internet, 27 October 2000, available from http://www.lasp.colorado.edu/stp/publications/galaxy.html. 2) CNN—subscription to this news service is only available via satellite or cable. 3) Christiana's live report from Europe requires a satellite link., 4) Weather Channel—meteorological pictures shown in the broadcast only available from weather satellites. In addition, the Weather Channel is only available via cable or satellite., 5) Security System—these systems were first developed for manned space flight to ensure the crew's health and safety. "NASA's role in the home and garden," 2; on-line, Internet, 2 November 2000, available from http://www.nasa.gov/women/garden/role.html. 6) Fire Alarm—these systems were also developed for manned space flight to ensure the crew's health and safety. "NASA's role in the home and garden," 2; on-line, Internet, 2 November 2000, available from http://www.nasa.gov/women/garden/ role.html and "Carbon Monoxide Detector," 2; on-line, Internet, 2 November 2000, available from http://www.nasa.gov/women/garden/safety.html. 7) NiCd battery—these high power batteries were developed in the space arena for use on satellites. Dennis Clark, "The Care and Feeding of NiCad Batteries," 5; on-line, Internet, 14 November 2000, available from http://38.232.238.4/1998/december/battery.html and Tony van Roon, "What About All Those NiCads," 7; on-line, Internet, 14 November 2000, available from http://www.uoguelph.ca/~antoon /hobby/nicad.htm. 8) Pager—communication satellites enable this technology. D.N. Baker et al., "Space Environmental Conditions During April and May 1998: An Indicator for the Upcoming Solar Maximum," 9; on-line, Internet, 27 October 2000, available from http://lasp.colorado.edu/stp/publications/galaxy.html. 9) Auto navigation system—this technology is becoming more prevalent and is made possible through the dual use of GPS satellites and Geographical Information Systems (GIS). GIS is greatly reliant on satellite remote sensing for on-orbit imaging. "Orbital to Outfit 50,000 Hertz Cars with GPS," 15 December 1998, 3; on-line, Internet, 9 November 2000,

http://www.spacedaily.com/news/orbsci-98q.html.   10)   International   video teleconference—much of the international telephone traffic goes over the oceans via communication satellites (it could also go via cable). 11) Gas quick pay—much of the telephony traffic is reliant on communication satellites to complete the link. "Galaxy 4 satellite not expected to be restored," 20 May 1998, 4; on-line, Internet, 27 October 2000, available from http://www.cnn.com/TECH/space/9805/20/satellite.update/. 12) German company via the Internet—international surfing can require communication links through satellites. 13) Vehicle Fleet tracking—NASA technology developed for astronomers is being used to aid companies to tracking their fleets. "NASA Technology Leads to Innovative Vehicle Tracking System," 25 June 1998, 3; on-line, Internet, 2 November 2000, available from http://nctn.hq.nasa.gov/success/msg00022.html. 14) Water Filters— NASA developed this convenience appliance for manned space flight. "NASA's role in the home and garden," 2; on-line, Internet, 2 November 2000, available from http://www.nasa.gov/women/garden/role.html.   15)   Virtual   Home   Viewing—"360- Degree Pictures," 2; on-line, Internet, 2 November 2000, available from http://www.nasa.gov /women/garden/entertai.html and "Home Shopping Made Easier," 2; on-line, Internet, 2 November 2000, available from http://www.nasa.gov/women/ garden/owner.html. 16) Snack Food—packaging for snack foods has its origin in the Apollo program. Mylar was one of the products used. "Food Packaging ," 2; on-line, Internet,   2   November   2000,   available   from http://www.nasa.gov/women/garden/kitchen.html. 17) Manual Trash Compactor—NASA developed this non-electrical compactor for use on the Space Shuttle. It is commercially available and is convenient for use in offices, boats and recreational vehicles. "Trash Compactor,"   2;   on-line,   Internet,   2   November   2000,   available   from http://nasa/gov/women/garden/kitchen.html. 18) Thermometer—the technology used to measure the temperature of stars is used in infrared thermometers that measure your temperature in your ear. "Infrared Thermometer," 2; on-line, Internet, 2 November 2000, available from http://www.nasa.gov/women/health/fromspac.html.   19) Blood pressure check—the familiar cuff that you slip your arm into at the doctor's office was developed to monitor the health of astronauts in space. "Your Blood Pressure", 2; on-line, Internet, 2 November 2000, available from http://www.nasa.gov/women/health/heart.html.   20) Mammography imaging—the same technology used to map distant stars is now used to more accurately map breast tissue. "Women's Outreach Initiative Welcome page," 2; on-line,   Internet,   2   November   2000,   available   from http://www.nasa.gov/women/welcomeContinued.html and "Hubble Fights Breast Cancer," March/April 1996, 2; on-line, Internet, 2 November 2000, available from htttp://nctn.hq.nasa.gov/innovation/Innovations4/HubbleFights.html.   21) Stereotactic Biopsy—this medical procedure extracts a sample with a needle rather than cutting into the tissue. This procedure is possible due to imaging technology designed for the Hubble Space Telescope. "Stereotactic Biopsy," 3; on-line, Internet, 2 November 2000, available from http//www.nasa.gov/women/health/cancer.html and "Medical Research," 3; on-line, Internet,   2   November   2000,   available   on http://liftoff.msfc.nasa.gov/station/science/benefits_med.html. 22) Laser angioplasty—in this procedure, a thin fiber optic catheter is insert into the blocked artery. The nonthermal laser then vaporizes the blockage. "Hall of Fame Honors Medical Spinoffs," June 1994, 2; on-line, Internet, 2 November 2000, available from http://nctn.hq.nasa.gov/innovation/Innovation23/MedicalSpinoffs.html and "Treating Heart Disease," 2; on-line, Internet, 2 November 2000, available from http://www.nasa.gov/women/health/heart.html. 23) Programmable pacemaker—these lifesavers incorporate three space technologies: spacecraft electrical power systems, microminiaturization for computer chips, and bi-directional telemetry for programming the pacemaker. "Programmable Pacemaker," 2, on-line, Internet, 2 November 2000, available from http://www.sti.nasa.gov/tto/spinoff1996/25.html. 24) Implanted defibrillator—this device senses irregular heartbeats and delivers an electrical stimulus to correct the heart beat. NASA's requirements for miniature electronics enabled this technology. "The Beat of Your Heart," 2; on-line, Internet, 2 November 2000, available from http://www.nasa.gov/women/health/heart/html. 25) Osteoporosis check—NASA is concerned about this condition since the same effect occurs on astronauts in space. NASA research has led to the development of a diagnosis tool, which does not require X-rays. "Osteoporosis," 2; on-line, Internet, 2 November 2000, available from http://www.nasa.gov/women/health/aging.html. 26) Lipstick with UV protection—NASA developed a thermoplastic to provide UV protection in space. This material can be added to cosmetics and exterior paints to provide UV protection. "NASA's 1999 Commercial Invention of the Year," 2; on-line, Internet, 2 November 2000, available from http://nctn.hq.nasa.gov/success/msg00025.html. 27) ParView Golf Carts—These carts are equipped with GPS receivers to locate the position of the golf cart and then the ProView system calculates the distance to the pin. "ParView scores with GPS for golf carts," 27 November 1998, 1, on-line, Internet, 16 November 2000, available from http://www.bizjournal.com/tampabay/stories/1998/11/23/daily10.html. 28) Credit card payment—increasingly, credit card approvals go over a satellite link. William B. Scott, "Cincspace: Focus More On Space Control," *Aviation Week and Space Technology*, November 13, 2000, 80. 29) Cellular phone call—increasingly, international phone calls are conducted over a satellite communications link vice a cable. 30) Jacket—insulation developed for spacecraft is now used in the clothing industry. This new material is better than wool and keeps a person dry even when it is wet. "Milk Bottle Blankets," 1; on-line, Internet, 2 November 2000, available from http://www.nasa.gov/women/garden/bath.html. 31) Personal lightning detection system—This commercial product is popular with homeowners, golfers, boaters and pilots. Space Shuttle tests of lightening detection lead to the development of this technology. "Storm Warning," 1, on-line, Internet, 2 November 2000, available from http://www.nasa.gov/women/garden/patio.html. 32) Home insulation—much of the energy efficiency products on the market today were developed by NASA for manned space flight. "Home Away From Home," 2; on-line, Internet, 2 November 2000, available from http://www.nasa.gov/women/garden/role.html. 33) Radiant barrier for homes—NASA developed this technology to shield the Apollo spacecraft from heat and cold. "Energy Efficiency," 2, on-line, Internet, 2 November 2000, available from http://www.nasa.gov/women/garden/energy.html. 34) Scratch-resistant glasses—space technology developed a highly abrasion-resistant coating to protect aerospace equipment from harsh environments. This technology has been shared with the commercial sun glasses industry. National Aeronautics and Space Agency, *Information Summaries Spinoffs*, February 1988. 35) Air conditioning sensors—developed by NASA for manned space flight. "Home Away From Home," 2; on-line, Internet, 2 November 2000, available from http://www.nasa.gov/women/garden/role.html. 36) Surround sound stereo—developed by NASA for manned space flight. "Home Away from Home," 2, on-line, Internet, 2 November 2000, available from http://www.nasa.gov/women/garden/role.html. 37) Stock Market trade—this routine activity is linked to orbiting spacecraft. William B. Scott, "Cincspace: Focus More On Space Control," *Aviation Week and Space Technology*, November 13, 2000, 80. 38) Distance learning—the link to provide live television classes often requires a satellite communications link. "Infosat Fast Facts," 2; on-line, Internet, February 2, 2001, available from http://www.infosat.com/presskit/infosat_facts.htm., 39) Automated Teller Machines (ATMs) Increasingly, ATMs are linked via satellites to the corporate office for financial transaction approvals. "Infosat Fast Facts," 2; on-line, Internet, February 2, 2001, available from http://www.infosat.com/presskit/infosat_facts.htm., 40) Sirius Satellite Radio provides 50 channels of commercial-free music and another 50 channels of news, sports, and entertainment for adults and children. These channels are available anywhere in the continental United States and this is made possible by three satellites. "Idea," 1; on-line, Internet, February 2, 2001, available from http://www.siriusradio.com/nonflash_site/idea.htm and "Frequently Asked Questions," 6; on-line, Internet, available from http://www.siriusradio.com/nonflash_site/faq.asp., 41) Movie Channel—this channel is only possible with cable or a satellite dish. With Direct TV, the satellite method is becoming increasingly common.

Chapter 3

A Day in the Life of America

One satellite loses contact with Earth and the lives of people all over North America are disrupted.[18]

It was a stark demonstration of the vulnerability of technology and just how dependent we have become on instant communication.[19]

Cable News Network
From two reports after the Galaxy IV failure
20 May 1998

The United States is the world's greatest exploiter of satellites with nearly three hundred currently on orbit.[20] This enabling force greatly aids American industry in dominating the global business world, which is becoming increasingly information centric. It was shown earlier that space assets are an essential part of each American's life but the same holds true for the nation as a whole. One way to objectively present this point of view is to quantify the impact to a nation if these space resources were not available.

On 19 May 1998, one of these three hundred satellites malfunctioned[21] and as a result, graphically illustrated the inextricable link between the vitality of American life and healthy satellites. When the Galaxy IV satellite failed, the American public quickly learned satellites are a vital part of their everyday life and without them they are severely inconvenienced. One of the first impacts was that untold millions of television and cable broadcast consumers, were not able to receive the service they counted on for business as

16

well as entertainment.[22] According to CNN, this loss of service was not confined to one network but included "CBS, ABC, CNN's Airport Network, [and] the WB Network."[23] These same untold millions were also denied their regular radio broadcasts. The largest radio broadcaster affected by this satellite malfunction was National Public Radio.[24] The fallout continued beyond television and radio and into the paging services sector. It is estimated that 45 million customers experienced a loss of pager service. To put this number in perspective, the Galaxy IV failure silenced nearly 80% of the United States' pagers.[25] Financial services were the final sector to be severely impacted. Bankcards were refused at countless fast-pay gas pumps since thousands of private networks were blanked out.[26] These networks were out of business because they relied on satellite communication links for bankcard purchase approvals. This outage was certainly a lesson on the criticality of satellites for the well being of this country. But, this was not the only time a satellite outage has caused a loss of prosperity and security. American's have witnessed other incidents with tangible impacts on national life.

In the summer of 1983, the Geostationary Operational Environmental Satellite (GOES) East satellite failed and was replaced by the GOES West satellite moved to take its place from its station over the Pacific. The National Weather Service felt justified in taking this action because in their mind, it was more important to track hurricanes and other weather on the east coast than to cover the central Pacific.[27] The consequence of moving this meteorological satellite to the east and not replacing it would be seen a year later. On Thanksgiving evening 1984, Hurricane Iwa slammed into the Hawaiian Islands of Oahu and Kauai. Earlier in the day, ships to the west of the islands warned of a hurricane forming and, as a result, a military plane was launched to locate and track it.

Unfortunately, the aircraft was not able to accurately locate it. While Hawaii knew the hurricane was coming, it did not have any precise information on the speed or direction. Hawaii was essentially "blind" to Iwa—a hurricane whose path had no historical precedent and which led right to the population centers.[28] While Iwa was unavoidable, Hawaii could have better prepared for this natural disaster had a replacement GOES west been put in place.

Satellite outages have affected more than just the weather services. But, on 13 June 1998, the primary control processor failed on a Galaxy VII communication satellite. As a result, several cable-television networks were down for a number of hours. Less than a month later, on July 4th, the control processor on a different communication satellite also failed. In this case, 3.7 million viewers of DirecTV were denied service. Fortunately, in both cases, satellite operators were able to switch to a backup processor and restore service.[29] In March 1999, another communication satellite experienced a control anomaly and as a consequence the North American operations of the Associated Press, among others, were disrupted for almost six hours.[30] These examples illustrate that when satellites fail, American life is affected. Entertainment, communications and vital information flows and services of all kinds are increasingly space dependent.

What is even more significant is that U.S. reliance on space is not diminishing, but rather growing. "Increasingly, phones, TV, radio, bank transactions, newspapers, credit card systems, etc., all depend upon [communication] satellites for some part of their link rather than being all ground based."[31] After the Galaxy IV breakdown, it was fortunate the satellite owner/operator promptly took corrective measures, by shifting signals within twenty-four hours, to avert continuing economic losses.[32] With these failures, one is tempted to jump to the preliminary conclusion that the U.S. ought not to depend so much on "fragile" satellites. However, at the time of the Galaxy IV failure, the overall industry loss for on-orbit satellites was less than one percent for the previous five years.[33] In addition, new communication satellite companies are pursuing on-orbit network architectures that will eliminate single point of failures.[34] These companies will mitigate satellite failures by routing around that failed node—just as phone companies do today with terrestrial networks. Teledesic and SkyCorp, for example, plan constellation sizes of 288 and 544, respectively, to ensure robust redundancy.[35] While it is clear that communication satellites are in demand, they are only one type of satellite vital to the nation's well being.

Another satellite system just as integral to America's well being is the Global Positioning System (GPS). Many people are familiar with the accurate navigation offered by this satellite constellation but fewer are aware of its ability to provide accurate timing. On first consideration, accurate timing would appear to only be relevant to laboratories. However, a thorough survey of precise timing applications proves just the opposite. Precise timing is required in "all communications systems; in most navigation systems; in computer systems and their networks; in accounting and banking systems; in traffic control systems; in much of scientific research; in fault detection and efficiency monitoring of power grids; in most military systems; in space research and explorations; in earth-quake detection and global plate tectonics; in environmental sensing; in ocean level and ocean current measurements; in air traffic control; collision avoidance and precision landing; and in truck fleet tracking and auto route mapping."[36] Increasingly, GPS is the source for this timing information due to its free and ubiquitous availability.

To understand the importance of GPS as a timing source, it is informative to review a March 1997 incident. Due to a small, manual input error on a routine update, one satellite, out of the constellation of twenty-four, broadcast a small timing error for six seconds. This error has little effect on navigation accuracy since a GPS receiver typically uses three to four satellites for a navigational fix. The same is not true for users only interested in timing. Those users get a "time hack" from the nearest satellite to synchronize their operations. Cellular phone companies are dependent on this timing source to manage their time-shared circuits. On 13 March, the cellular network on the eastern United States picked up this error and as a result, 110 out of 800 cellular sites crashed for a good many hours.[37]

While satellite failures are not uncommon and their impacts significant, most people today do not recall them. This would not be the case if these satellites were more broadly attacked for greater effect. With almost every satellite unprotected, the very infrastructure of this nation would come to a near halt with a hostile attack. One has only to recall the many uses for communication, meteorological and GPS satellites to imagine the impact from the loss of these services. The consequences would be even greater if all classes of satellites were attacked, since satellites are woven into the very fabric of our society. Replacement of these assets would be excruciatingly slow since this nation lacks a rapid reconstitution capability. Moreover, the price tag for many of these satellites is exorbitant—several hundred million dollars a piece. Finally, most satellites are not mass-produced and not easily replaced, even if the capital and booster were available to replace them. The national recovery would be a long, slow process that could easily take over a year for a fairly limited attack. The recently completed space commission calls this possible scenario a "Space Pearl Harbor."[38]

One final note concerning hostile attacks. It is a threat that is already a reality. The threat can be minor such as the hacking of "Captain Midnight" into an HBO broadcast in 1986. In this case, the attack was only a nuisance; he interrupted a movie with a printed message protesting the scrambling of the HBO signal.[39] A more extreme attack would involve the actual degradation or destruction of a satellite. In 1988, the U.S. intelligence agencies reported that Soviet ground lasers had damaged U.S. spy satellites, monitoring Soviet nuclear missiles. The report went on to state the growing fear in the Intelligence Community that other U.S. reconnaissance satellites would come under increasing attack due the Soviets' construction of six new laser battle stations.[40] Imagine the risks if the U.S. had been "blind in space," but this time facing the looming "hurricane" of nuclear ICBMs.

Before addressing how to prevent such a catastrophic event from occurring, it is necessary to first gain a better understanding of American dependence on space derived information, both in business as well as the military.

Notes

[18] "Galaxy 4 satellite not expected to be restored," 20 May 1998, 4; on-line, Internet, 27 October 2000, available from http://www.cnn.com/TECH/space/9805/20/satellite.update/.

[19] "Why did satellite Galaxy 4 go off course?," 20 May 1998, 3; on-line, Internet, 27 October 2000, available from http://www.cnn.com/TECH/space/9805/20/satellite.explainer/.

[20] Need reference and also total number on orbit and next highest country.

[21] D.N. Baker et al., "Pager Satellite Failure May Have Been Related to Disturbed Space Environment," 6 October 1998, 8; on-line, Internet, 27 October 2000, available from http://www.agu.org/sci_soc/articles/eisbaker.html.

Notes

[22] "Galaxy 4 Meltdown: A Small Foretaste of The Millennium Bug; Where's Al?," 21 May 1998, 2; on-line, Internet, 27 October 2000, available from http//www.security-policy.org/papers/1998/98-C88.html.

[23] "Galaxy 4 satellite not expected to be restored."

[24] Ibid.

[25] Baker. This "45 million" number was also quoted in USA Today, p. 1, 21 May 1998.

[26] "Galaxy 4 satellite not expected to be restored."

[27] Bob Cunningham, "Some postscript notes about Hurricane Iwa," March 5, 1987, 2; on-line, Internet, February 9, 2001, available from http://catless.ncl.ac.uk/Risks/4.56.html.

[28] Bob Cunningham, "Hurricane Iwa and the Hawaii blackout of 1984," February 17, 1987, 2; on-line, Internet, February 9, 2001, available from http://catless.ncl.ac.uk/Risks/4.51.html.

[29] Bleeding Edge, "More satellite problems," July 12, 1998, 1; on-line, Internet, February 9, 2001, available from http://catless.ncl.ac.uk/Risks/19.85.html.

[30] Doneel Edelson, "Satellite o5tage cuts news service," March 12, 1999, 1; on-line, Internet, available from http://catless.ncl.ac.uk/Risks/20.25.html.

[31] D. N. Baker et al., "Space Environmental Conditions During April and May 1998: An Indicator for the Upcoming Solar Maximum," 9; on-line, Internet, 27 October 2000, available from http://www.lasp.colorado.edu/stp/publications/galaxy.html.

[32] "Galaxy 4 satellite not expected to be restored."

[33] "Galaxy 4 satellite not expected to be restored."

[34] On a side note, a Galaxy telecommunication satellite failed on 22 November 2000. Since it was functioning as a backup, none of the full-time customers were affected by the outage. For the full report, see "U.S. Galaxy 7 television satellite lost in space," *Spaceflight Now*, 25 November 2000, 3; on-line, Internet, 28 November 2000, available from http://www.spacflightnow.com/news/n0011/25galaxy7/.

[35] "Teledesic," 4; on-line, Internet, 30 October 2000, available from http://www.teledesic.com/tech/tech.htm and Leander Kahney, "Internet Satellite Going Cheap," 14 June 2000, 3; on-line, Internet, 13 November 2000, available from http://www.wired.com/news/technology/0,1282,36964,00.html.

[36] David W. Allen, "The Impact of Precise Time in Our Lives: A Historical and Futuristic Perspective Surrounding GPS," 9; on-line, Internet, February 6, 2001, available from http://www.allanstime.com/Publications/DWA/IONGPS95/.

[37] Simon P. Worden, "Space Control for the 21st Century, A Space "Navy" Protecting the Commercial Basis of America's Wealth," in *Spacepower for a New Millennium, Space and U.S. National Security*, ed. Peter L. Hayes et al. (New York: MacGraw-Hill Companies, Inc, 2000), 228.

[38] The Commission used this phrase to convey the growing vulnerability of the U.S. space assets. With U.S.'s dependence on space growing each year and with little protection on board the satellites, space assets present an inviting target just waiting to be attacked—very similar to the Navy's fleet harbored in Pearl Harbor before WWII.

Notes

Commission to Assess United States National Security Space Management and Organization, Executive Summary, January 11, 2001, 13.

[39] The following source contains a copy of the Federal Communications Commission's 22 July 1986 news release on this subject. "Captain Midnight's raid on HBO," July 26, 1986, 3; on-line Internet, March 26, 2001, available from http://www.totse.com/en/media/cable_and_satellite_television_hacks/captainm.html.

[40] Peter G. Neumann, "U.S. Fears Satellites Damaged," January 24, 1988, 1; on-line, Internet, February 9, 2001, available from http://catless.ncl.ac.uk/Risks/6.13.html.

Chapter 4

Space: Enabler for American Business

... just as oil drives the engine of today's industrial society, space will drive the engine of tomorrow's information society. As an emerging center of gravity, space capabilities impact almost every industry ...[41]

General Howell M. Estes III
Commander in Chief, United States Space Command
Remarks in congressional testimony
1998

American business is moving quickly to take advantage of space assets' unique capabilities. The race is on to rapidly advance and integrate these capabilities into today's business operations to maximize their competitive edge in the global information economy. This race is not only about exploiting orbiting satellites but also all of the associated spin-off technologies. The space arena incorporates many of the important areas of high technology: "software development, chip technology, sophisticated electronics, telecommunications, satellite manufacturing, life sciences, advanced materials, and launch technology."[42] With this technology, space becomes very appealing in today's information age—space is lucrative way to provide unique services. As a result, space is big business. The global space marketplace has grown into an annual $100 billion industry. In addition, the "space industry directly employs more than 800,000 people and is expanding at a rate of 40,000 jobs per year."[43]

One company that typifies this race to exploit space is 3M. In December of 1983, the top 3M executives met to map out how their long-range research center would remain competitive through the end of the century. The research lab's director briefed several technical problems that his scientists were not able to crack and proposed conducting a series of experiments on the Space Shuttle to advance the research. The chairman of the board gave his full approval and thus, 3M became the first major corporation, other than an aerospace company with NASA contracts, to push space-based research and development. Two months later a memorandum of understanding was signed between NASA and 3M. By the summer of 1984, 3M was building the space experiment and by September, they delivered the hardware for flight checkout. In November, the experiment flew into space. 3M achieved the unprecedented, going from agreement to flight in nine months compared to the three years nominally required by experienced aerospace contractors. Over the next two years, a series of follow-on experiments were conducted and in late 1986, 3M signed an agreement with NASA to receive sixty-two free experiments on the Shuttle over the next ten years. As for the discoveries made from this research, 3M is not willing to tip their hands to their competitors and NASA is honoring this secrecy.[44]

3M is not the only company using space technology to advance the bottom line. American business in general depends on over one hundred and fifty satellites to maintain their competitive edge. The vast majority of these space assets are communication satellites but there is also a growing market for remote sensing (imaging) satellites.[45] The commercial world is also reliant on the Global Positioning System (GPS) satellites even though they are owned and operated by the Department of Defense.

All of these space systems speed the flow of vital information to near-instantaneous rates, allowing companies to reach out further, faster, cheaper and more effectively than ever before. As a result, companies are more closely connected to their customers as well as potential customers.

Communication satellites are becoming an integral part of American business. This is due, in large part, to companies relying on telephony services to conduct business and satellites increasing carrying this type of communication. These satellites speed the flow of information and thus the rate at which business is being conducted. One small example of these near instantaneous communication rates is credit card telephony approvals. Using terrestrial communication paths, it takes from 15-30 seconds for an approval to reach the business. With satellite links, this small but essential part of American business can be cut to about 5 seconds.[46] In addition to credit card transactions, communication satellites help underpin telephones, cellular phones, video conferencing, Internet, data transmission, TV, radio, bank transactions, newspapers, credit card approval systems, stock market transactions, live distance learning, fleet tracking, and paging services. As a result of this diversity of applications, the communication satellite market is the largest and most profitable market in the space arena.[47]

Remote sensing satellites are also being used by American business. Applications include weather forecasting, damage assessment of natural disasters, ozone depletion monitoring, city planning using geographic information systems, tracking of icebergs, location of natural resources, ocean monitoring and pollution monitoring. One application that we all profit from is agricultural crop monitoring or "precision farming."

With remote sensing, a farmer is able to monitor the health and growth of his crops. Based on this information, the farmer is able to fertilize, water and control insect problems more accurately. With this improved accuracy, the farmer makes better use of his expendables and thus is more competitive in the global market. At harvest time, remote-sensing data can further help the farmer by predicting the size of yield as well as when it is optimal to pick the produce. The consumer ultimately profits with better produce at a lower price.[48] Some California vineyards are fully exploiting the current potential of space resources to better husband their fields. In addition to monitoring the fields via remote sensing, each individual vine is cataloged with GPS coordinates. The "care and feeding" of the field is now tailored down to each discrete plant.[49]

There are four salient points to draw from this agricultural illustration. The first is that this application of remote sensing data may appear too high tech for the average farmer. Nothing could be farther from the truth. American farmers are increasingly turning to space technology to produce more with less. This motivation is based in part on the impending loss of government subsidies in 2002.[50] The bottom line is that remote sensing satellites deliver the information needed to keep American farmers competitive. The second relevant point is that this is not a case of the government seeking to increase the use of LANDSAT data. Rather, this is a new and growing market that already has four players from private industry: Space Imaging, Earthwatch, Orbview, and Resource 21.[51] A third point is that the quality of information is approaching "surgical precision." In the past, farmers relied on LANDSAT imagery that only had a resolution of 15, 30 or 60 meters.[52] Today, one-meter resolution imagery is commercially available for any spot on the globe; all you need is a credit card and an Internet connection. If that is not good enough, half-meter technology is already in the works.[53] What is significant about this quality of information is that until former President Clinton authorized the commercial development of this technology, this resolution was reserved for U.S. spy satellites. When this overhead imagery is combined with the accuracy of GPS, farmers can truly assess how the "patient" is doing and diagnose the appropriate cure for their fields, plant by plant if they wish. The fourth and final point is that the consumer and the farmer are not the only ones who profit from this data. The stock market is also a player in using this information. With remote sensing data, analysts are better able to predict futures on American crops and thus are savvier in their market trades. The benefits do not stop at the domestic level. With remote sensing satellites flying unimpeded over all regions of the globe, accurate crop forecasting information is available on any country of interest. In short, market projections of future crops, and hence modulation of supply and demand for global production is possible. Armed with this information, American negotiators are better able to get the "best deal" since they know the status of the country's crops. In the early 1990's, the U.S. government used remote sensing information from satellites to accurately assess the state of the Russian crops. Based on this knowledge, the U.S. provided grain to Russia to ensure it did not further collapse.[54] This "agricultural spying" is not restricted to only U.S. trade negotiators. Rather, this information can also help American businesses in purchasing agricultural products from foreign markets at the best price. The world will become increasingly smaller as the utilization of space assets increases. As the foreign remote sensing satellite market increases, this competitive edge will decrease since other countries will be able to assess American crop yields.

American business not only profits from on-orbit space assets but also from spin-off space technology. One field that has been greatly advanced by the study of manned space flight is medicine. When astronauts return from space they experience certain physiological disorders that also occur with aging: "cardiovascular deconditioning, balance disorders, weakening bones and muscles, disturbed sleep, and depressed immune response."[55] NASA's Life Science's Program is making headway in each of these areas and this new information is passed along to the medical community to enhance the health care for aging people. NASA is also helping the pharmaceutical industry develop new drugs for treating cancer, diabetes, emphysema, and immune system disorders.[56] A final spin-off technology that is aiding the medical community is digital imaging. This technology was developed in the 1960s for exploration of the Earth's Moon. This technology is being refined at the Stennis Space Center to enhance CAT scans, ultra-sound images, and X-ray pictures. This same technology is used during brain and heart angioplasty and for surgical monitoring.[57] These three examples are by no means an exhaustive list of the medical spinoffs from space, but rather illustrate how space information is vital to the advancement of medicine.

The medical field is not the only field that profits from space technology. Several other fields do so as well. These include: microelectronics, battery advances, home security systems, entertainment systems, snack food packaging, weather forecasting, water recycling, scratch-resistant lens, flame resistant materials, advanced aircraft engines, flame resistant materials, anti-corrosion paint, outer garments and breathing apparatus for workers in hazardous environments, vehicle controller for the handicapper, speech autocuer, voice-controlled wheelchair, reading machine for the blind, and energy efficient materials for home construction as well as clothes. In 1988, NASA reported that there are over 30,000 spinoffs or applications of space technology.[58] In addition to "spin-off" applications, advances in space technology also cause a chain reaction in creating "spin-on" breakthroughs. These advances are the logical follow on into new applications and markets that only result from the original breakthrough. The number of spin-offs and spin-ons will only continue to grow as America increases its command of space and thus strengthening its position in the global marketplace. All of these applications illustrate the point that American business can not survive with out the competitive edge space resources bring. Space technology is aiding the flow of information as well as the creation of new information. This pattern of symbiosis in the public and private sectors, for business, government, the scientific community, medicine, agriculture, education, entertainment and the military is enabled by space. We now turn to the military aspect.

Notes

[41] General Howell M. Estes, Commander in Chief, United States Space Command, address to Congressional Committee, Washington D.C., 1998, 17; on-line, Internet, 27 October 2000, available from http://sac.saic.com/space/docs/speeches/speech9.htm.

[42] Keith Cahoun-Senghor, Director, Office of Air & Space Commercialization, U.S. Department of Commerce, "Trends in Commercial Space 1996," 2; on-line, Internet, 13 October 2000, available from http://www.ta.doc.gov/space/tics/intro-text.htm.

[43] Quoted in Jennifer DeButts, "Lead, Follow, or Get Out of the Way: The Case for Privatizing NASA," 12; on-line, Internet, 2 November 2000, available from http://www.ntu.org/issues/spend/domestic/pp121.htm.

[44] David Gump, *Space Enterprise: beyond NASA* (New York: Praeger Publishers, 1990), 125-127, 134.

[45] These two classes of satellites are the primary ones owned and operated by American businesses. However, there are additional satellites on orbit: military, intelligence, scientific, and deep space probes.

[46] Not only is this satellite service faster, it is also very affordable. The monthly rate per location is $75 per month plus ThruComm terminals. Linda Sakelaris, "ThruComm offers retailers wireless POS," 2; on-line, Internet, November 21, 2000, available from http://www.telekomnet.com/writer_linda/5-22-00_thrucomm_pos.asp?print=-1.

[47] Peter L. Hayes et al. "Spacepower for a New Millennium, Examining Current U.S. Capabilities and Policies," in *Spacepower for a New Millennium, Space and U.S.*

Notes

National Security, ed. Peter L. Hayes et al. (New York: MacGraw-Hill Companies, Inc, 2000), 2.

[48] "In the Kitchen," 2; on-line, Internet, 2 November 2000, available from http://www.nasa.gov/women/kitchen/html and "In the garden and on the farm," 2; on-line, Internet, 2 November 2000, available from http://www.nasa.gov/women/garden/farm.html.

[49] Dr. Grant Hammond, Air War College Faculty, interviewed by author, 12 January 2001.

[50] William J. Hudson, "New Satellite Application in Agriculture," November 20, 1997, 3; on-line, Internet, 30 October 2000, available from http://www.intellectualcapital.com/issues/97/1120/icguested2.asp.

[51] Ibid.

[52] "LANDSAT 7 Facts," 3, on-line, Internet, February 8, 2001, available from http://www.geo.arc.nasa.gov/sge/landsat/17.html.

[53] In December 2000, the U.S. government gave permission for EarthWatch to operate imaging satellites capable of half-meter resolution. Quickbird 2 will be launched in October 2001 and will be capable of three feet resolution. Jason Bates, "EarthWatch to Sharpen Its Images," March 22, 2001, 2; on-line, Internet, March 27, 2001, available from

http://www.space.com/businesstechnology/technology/earthwatch_quickbird_010322.html.

[54] Col. Ted Hailes, Air War College faculty, interviewed by author, 16 January 2001.

[55] "Parallel Processes? The Study of Human Adaptation to Space Helps us Understand Aging," 3; on-line, Internet, November 2, 2000, available from http://www.quest.arc.nasa.gov/space/challenge/background/pp.html.

[56] "Medical Research," 3; on-line Internet, November 2, 2000, available from http://www.liftoff.msfc.nasa.gov/station/science/benefits_med.html.

[57] "Technology Transfer, Hall of Fame Honors Medical Spinoffs," May/June 1994, 2; on-line, Internet, November 2, 2000, available from http://www.nctn.hq.nasa.gov/innovation/Innovation23/MedicalSpinoffs.html.

[58] National Aeronautics and Space Agency, *Information Summaries Spinoffs*, February 1988.

Chapter 5

Space: Enabler for American Military

In terms of using space assets, this was probably the best we've done—surely superior to Desert Storm from everything we can learn. But there's still a long way to go before space is really integrated with the rest of the campaign.[59]

General Richard Meyers
Commander, U.S. Space Command
April 2000

Practically every piece of information used by the U.S. military today is either derived from or transmitted through space.[60]

Lt. Gen. Donald G. Cook
Vice Commander, Air Force Space Command
September 1999

The world readily acknowledges the American military as the preeminent military power. This military might combined with America's economic power are the main reasons for the U.S. emerging from the Cold War as the only superpower. How did the U.S. military achieve such a success? One could argue that in the 1990's space technology and the inherent information flow played a substantial role in this result. Just as U.S. business vitally depends on space assets for a competitive advantage, so the U.S. military also relies on space capabilities as a force enabler. Today the military depends on space assets to provide five missions: communications, navigation, early warning, weather and intelligence. All of these missions are important types of information on which we are increasingly dependent for military superiority. The important key to recognize is that space and information are inextricably linked. The two are not synonymous but having one without the other is indeed rare and becoming more so every day. When the time dimension of these real-time or near real-time critical, information flows are added for consideration, the importance of space-based assets for all these missions becomes even more significant. A review of the Kosovo crisis reveals just how space-dependent the military is for military supremacy.

The Kosovo crisis was chosen since it was the last major engagement by the U.S. military and as such illustrates the current dependency on space and rapid information. Due to the air nature of the campaign, many of the advantages enabled by space were only apparent for combat air applications. Even so, one need only review the DESERT STORM report to Congress to appreciate that space systems equally enable ground and maritime ops.[61]

Like the commercial community, the military's greatest use of space assets is for the communication mission. Satellite communication allows the military to deploy to any hotspot in the world and still remain in contact with the leadership, whether it is the National Command Authorities or the local, in-theater headquarters. Satellite communications are not a static requirement for military operations, but rather one that is growing as the military increasingly takes advantage of information technologies. General Mike Ryan, Chief of Staff of the Air Force, recently reported that the amount of bandwidth required for ALLIED FORCE was five times the amount required for DESERT STORM. This extensive network connected 40 different locations in 15 countries. While some of this network used landlines, much of it was only made possible through the use of satellites.[62] Of all the spaceborne communications used in Kosovo, eighty percent of it traveled over commercial systems.[63] It is evident that the military's demand exceeds its own supply.

Another critical space resource for the military is the Global Positioning System (GPS). The requirement for GPS data grew from ALLIED FORCE to DESERT STORM. This demand resulted from weather that at times wrecked havoc with laser and optical guided munitions. With GPS munitions, the Air Force was able to conduct strike missions even if weather obscured the target. Perhaps the best example of this all-weather capability was the B-2 weapon system. With B-2's armed with Joint Direct Attack Munitions, the USAF was able to conduct all weather attacks around the clock. The bottom line is that the B-2, the Air Force's most expensive aircraft, would have been an irrelevant weapon system without GPS. The Air Force was not the only service that relied on GPS for strike operations. The Navy's Tomahawk cruise missile also used satellite-aided navigation as the primary method to navigate to the target.[64] Another benefit derived from the GPS constellation was accurate timing. With GPS timing, the commanders were able to synchronize data links among AWACS, JSTARS, Rivet Joint, UAVs and data fusion centers.[65] This synchronization of information allowed commanders to maintain dominant battlespace awareness and thus make quicker, better-informed decisions.

The Defense Support Program—a constellation of strategic missile warning satellites—was another key space system used in Kosovo. This system was pressed into service to provide near-real time battle damage assessment on bomber and cruise missile strikes. Armed with this data the air campaign planners were able to assess attack effectiveness and begin building future strike packages.[66] Once again, satellites increased the speed of information, consequently allowing the commanders to maintain a high ops tempo with a rapid retargeting/replanning cycle.

Perhaps the most revolutionary use of space systems in Kosovo was the incorporation of the Multi-Source Tactical System into the cockpits of our bombers.[67] This system displayed space-derived information (intelligence) to include "near real-time information of threats, position and status of other friendly platforms, mission rehearsal data and updated target parameters and imagery."[68] This system proved to be so successful that on several missions, the commanders were able to retarget sorties en-route.[69] This system allowed the first-ever CAS push for B-1s.[70] Rapid information allowed the optimization of weapon systems used in combat and thus enabled a shorter Observe-Orient-Decide-Act (OODA) loop.

The final space systems used in Kosovo were weather satellites. Today the majority of data used for weather forecasting is derived from weather satellites. This information allows for a clearer picture of the battlespace and therefore allows a commander to minimize the impact of the weather on combat operations. Even with the information provided by satellites, this "fog of war" was not totally eliminated. The allied air forces only experienced 21 days of good weather out of the 78-day air campaign and this resulted in sixteen percent of all strike sorties being lost to weather.[71] Until we are able to control the weather, these satellites will continue to play a major role in combat operations.

All told, four dozen satellites from nearly two dozen countries were used to wage war in the Balkans. "It was the largest armada of spacecraft ever brought to bear on a single war in history."[72] This armada allowed unprecedented information superiority for the commanders and was a harbinger of the way future conflicts will be fought.

Space assets and the rapid information that they bring are key prerequisites to successful combat operations. Former Secretary of Defense Cohen made this absolutely clear in his *2000 Annual Report to the President*. In this report, he links information superiority and space assets as the force multiplier for today's reduced-size military. He points out that the information superiority realized in Kosovo produced enhanced mission effectiveness and improved efficiencies in the form of "increased speed of command, a higher tempo of operations, greater lethality, less fratricide and collateral damage, increased survivability, streamlined combat support, and more effective force synchronization."[73]

While the United States' military currently enjoys the fruits of space superiority, it would be wise not to rest on these laurels. In DESERT STORM, the world took note of the role space played in the awesome power wrought by the coalition air forces. General Myers, as Commander in Chief of U.S. Space Command, argues that Slobadan Milosevic learned from Saddam Hussein's mistake and as a result built a credible air defense system.[74] One need only recall an that F-117, arguably the Air Force's most high-tech fighter, was shot down. What Milosevic did not focus attention on was disrupting our military's access to space assets. Again the world learned that if the U.S. maintains it space superiority in combat; it will most likely win over its opponent. With this lesson readily apparent, future adversaries "will modify their forces to try and deny our space superiority."[75] To remain the world's space and information superpower, our space infrastructure must be expanded and protected, both in the commercial and government arenas. A review of European powers, in the past millennium, demonstrates the principles of expansion, protection, as well as private and government investment were the source of national power.

Notes

[59] *Initial Report – The Air War over Serbia, Aerospace Power in Operation Allied Force*, (United States Air Forces in Europe, Studies and Analysis Directorate, April 2000), 53.

[60] Lieutenant General Donald G. Cook, "Royal United Services Institute for Defense Studies Military Utility of Space Conference Keynote Address," Whitehall, London, September 8, 1999, 6; on-line, Internet, November 28, 2000, available from http://www.spacecom.af.mil/hqafspc/library/speeches/royal_inst.htm.

[61] Department of Defense, *Conduct of the Persian Gulf Conflict, Final Report to Congress: Pursuant to Title V Persian Gulf Conflict Supplemental Authorization and Personnel Benefits Act of 1991 (Pubic Law 102-25) Chapters I through VIII* (April 1992).

[62] Peter Grier, "The Investment on Space," February 2000, 8; on-line, Internet, October 27, 2000, available from http://www.afa.org/magazine/0200investment.html.

[63] Ibid.

[64] General Richard B. Myers, Command in Chief, U.S. Space Command, "Space Superiority is Fleeting," January 1, 2000, 3; on-line, Internet, November 30, 2000, available from http//www.spacecom.af.mil/usspace/avweek-gen%20meyers. htm.

[65] Lieutenant General Cook.

[66] General Ralph Eberhart, "Statement of General Ralph E. Eberhart, USAF Command in Chief North American Aerospace Defense Command and United States Space Command Before the United States Senate Armed Services Strategic Subcommittee," March 8, 2000, 11, on-line, Internet, November 28, 2000, available from http://www.spacecom.af.mil/usspace/cinc8mar00.htm.

[67] Cook.

[68] General Eberhart.

[69] Cook.

[70] The 76 SOPS was the squadron that pushed the implementation of MSTS in ALLIED FORCE. Lt. Col. Dave Ziegler, 76 SOPS/CC, Peterson AFB, CO, provided this information while reviewing a draft of this paper, 12 March 2001.

[71] Major General David F. MacGhee, "Emerging Concepts on AF Employment," lecture, Air War College, Maxwell Air Force Base, AL., 7 December 2000.

[72] "The Satellite War over Yugoslavia," 3; on-line, Internet, February 13, 2001, available from http://www.spacetoday.org/Satellites/YugoWarSats.html.

[73] Secretary of Defense William S. Cohen, Annual Report to the President and Congress, 2000, 21; on-line, Internet, November 30, 2000, available from http://www.dtic.mil/execsec/adr2000/chap8.html.

[74] General Meyers.

[75] Meyers.

Chapter 6

THE PAST

The Quest For Knowledge and Wealth

[The British East India Company] accomplished a work such as in the whole history of the human race no other company ever attempted and as such is ever likely to attempt in the years to come.[76]

Report in the *Times* after 274 years of business, which peaked with the domination of all trade in Asia, Africa, and America
1874

History is replete with nations expanding knowledge and wealth to increase their prosperity and thus their power in the international arena. The most successful countries were not deterred even though the costs were exorbitant both in terms of money and men. Increased knowledge enabled the promise of wealth, which served as a guiding light and helped to sustain these nations even in the midst of arduous hardships and hostile climates. For those who succeeded, the result was a rise to becoming a global or regional power. This success profited all, both the nation and its people. Once a source of wealth was exploited, nations defended these sources with military might for to do otherwise would result in their loss of international power and the lifestyle to which they had become accustomed. It is a timeless cycle—knowledge, exploitation, investment, consumption, and protection—and history is full of such examples, some of which are reviewed below.

Venice: Rise of a Regional Power

The rise and fall of European powers in the last millennium serve as a good record of the quest for wealth and the auspicious consequences. At the beginning of the second millennium, the city-state of Venice was well on its way to dominating trade in the Mediterranean. This domination was not mere happenstance but was rather the result of a consistent policy for several centuries. Venetian policy sought to increase wealth through the use of sea power vice through the acquisition of territory. The wars they fought supported this overarching political objective. When they did win, the political settlements always resulted in arrangements that were detrimental to rival sea powers, which further secured Venice's established trade in Levantine waters and which gained new trading privileges thus allowing commercial expansion into new areas. As early as the ninth century, the Venetians began to build large military ships for the express purpose of guarding lagoon entrances from trading rivals.[77] By the tenth century, the Venetians were using economic (e.g. boycotts) and military instruments of power to further protect their source of wealth and power. As a result, they were the dominant merchants and carriers in the area.[78]

During the eleventh century the number and wealth of Venetians continued to grow.[79] They excelled as the middlemen in a growing trade between Europe and other countries in the Mediterranean. From Greece, they exported wine, oil, fruit and nuts to Egypt and returned with wheat, beans and sugar. Western Europe was producing more and more metal wares and woolen cloth that were in demand in the Levant (Crete,

Cyprus, Syria and Palestine) and this allowed the Europeans to buy more products from the East. From Romania, the Venetians brought back raw silk, silk material, alum, red dyes, wax, honey, cotton, wheat, furs and slaves.[80] From the Levant, they imported pepper, cinnamon, cloves, nutmeg, and ginger that were in high demand since there was little refrigeration. From Palestine and Syria, the exportable merchandise included lemons, oranges, almonds, figs, cotton, silks and sugar.[81] Bales of eastern drugs and spices came from the Far East via the Red Sea.[82] To protect this thirteenth century "growth market," the Venetians conquered Constantinople—securing trade in the Black Sea,[83] creating a naval base in Crete and establishing their presence in the port of Acre.[84] In 1330, Venetian naval power expanded with a separate squadron dedicated to the protection of commerce in the Gulf while the main war fleet patrolled in the Aegean Sea or eastern Mediterranean.[85] Much of Venice's wealth was attributable to their "command of the sea." While the Venetians were not able to sweep the entire Mediterranean they did establish "command" in the Adriatic.[86] Their aim was to provide protection for their merchant convoys and "to send support to colonies while inflicting losses on the trade of an enemy or raiding his coasts or colonies."[87] However, the Venetian "command of the sea" was not to last.

Genoa: Rise of a Peer Competitor

After 1250, Venice's access to the Levant region was fiercely contested by the city-state of Genoa. Beginning in 1100, Genoa had increased its wealth through plundering in the western Mediterranean where it was not in direct competition with Venice. Up to this point, the Genoese employed a "hit and run" approach that proved to be highly effective in their quest for wealth.[88] Over time, they transitioned from a new sea power—one focused on pirating or privateering—to a mature sea power—one concerned with maintaining lines of communication and protecting maritime trade.[89] As they began to expand their commercial trading into the eastern Mediterranean, they came into direct competition with the Venetians. In 1258, the first naval battle between these two city-states occurred. The Venetians scored an overwhelming victory by destroying half of the Genoese fleet. In 1263 and again in 1266, the two naval powers clashed and again, Venice emerged as the victor. Though victorious, the naval wars were proving costly to the Venetians. In addition, Venice was suffering from the resumption of Genoese "cut and run" tactics on Venetian shipping.[90] From this time on, there was a constant struggle to control trade and so the Venetians and Genoese fought whenever their ships met. Over time, privateering was proving more profitable than convoying and for this reason, the Venetians sought peace. The Genoese were slow to come to the negotiations table— since they were making out better than the Venetians—and it was only through King Louis IX of France that both agreed to an uneasy peace in 1270.[91]

The Genoese continued their naval and economic expansion for the next twenty five years. In the Tyrrhenian Sea they were the undisputed naval power. They expanded their trading to Bruges and England and in the Black Sea and Asia Minor.[92] From 1270-90, Venice also grew in power. Its industrial output increased and Venice made the most of enforcing her position in the Adriatic. Over time, Venice replaced "Constantinople as the chief market for the raw materials from … Romania, such as wine, wax, oil, honey, cotton, wool, and hides, and also as the manufacturing center from which they received supplies."[93] As competition increased, both Venice and Genoa sought to expel each other from the Black Sea. In the 1290s, there were several skirmishes with both sides winning and losing. During this time, neither navy concentrated on convoy protection but rather focused on raiding each other's colonies.[94] The war fleets finally met, force on force in 1298. In this war, the Genoese displayed better seamanship, maneuver, and combat and so won the conflict. In 1299, both sides agreed to settle their differences and peacefully divide Mediterranean trading.[95] Over the next decades internal strife began to grow in Genoa. This power struggle, along with a reemerging rivalry with Venice, began to sap the strength of the city-state. In 1380, the two naval powers met again in conflict. This time the Venetians struck a blow from which Genoa never recovered. Over the following years, Genoa began to lose its overseas possessions and its naval power was no longer a force to be reckoned with.[96] Venice had overcome its peer competitor once and for all— it would not face another commercial war with Genoa.[97] To the victor goes the spoils and in this case, the prize was a trade monopoly in the eastern Mediterranean. As a result, Venice's position as a regional power was reestablished. Their reign was not to last, however, a new competitor lay waiting with an asymmetric attack.

Portugal: Quest for a Monopoly in the East

In any profitable marketplace, there will always be competitors seeking ever-larger shares of the available wealth. Portugal's quest for wealth began somewhat serendipitously in the fifteenth century when King John sought an opportunity for his sons and other knights to display acts of gallantry. The King decided the best option to display their Christian valor was to launch a Crusade against Ceuta, "a Muslim stronghold and trading center on the African side opposite Gibraltar."[98] On 24 August 1415, the Portuguese began their crusade against Ceuta. The Muslims were overwhelmed in less than one day and by afternoon the Portuguese were looting the city.

This new found treasure gave the Portuguese their first taste of the riches of Africa and the East Indies. In addition to gold, silver, and jewels, the Crusaders found rich tapestries, oriental rugs, exotic spices and the essentials of life: wheat, rice, and salt. At the time of this conquest, Ceuta was a bustling city of twenty four thousand shops selling wares of gold, silver, brass, silks, and spice brought by the caravans from the East Indies and Saharan Africa. However, with Ceuta now a "Christian" city, the Portuguese killed the goose that laid the golden egg—the city was now profitless since the caravans no longer arrived. At this point in history, Portugal faced a strategic decision—to make peace with the local tribes or continue their exploration where no European had traveled.[99]

Portugal chose the latter course of action as the most rewarding and so embarked on a century-and-a-half venture. This long-term planning was only possible because the nation as a whole shared this collaborative commitment. With a clearly defined purpose and the required national support, the Portuguese were on their way to success.[100] By the 1470s, the national policy was bearing fruit. At this time the Portuguese had established trade with the tribes on Africa's Gold Coast and were regularly taking vast amounts of gold back to Europe.[101] To further speed the rate of exploration and the rate of wealth building, King Alfonso V took the unprecedented measure of incentivizing discovery. Up until this point, the rate of exploration had been slow due to sea captains' superstitions. By committing to explore a given distance in a given amount of time, the sea captain was given a monopoly on all the new trade of which the King was given a share.[102]

In 1488 Bartolomeu Dias circumnavigated the southern tip of Africa.[103] The round trip took over sixteen months, at a cost of several lives, and yet the Portuguese still pressed on.[104] A decade later, Vasco da Gama's sailed all the way from Portugal to India in eleven months.[105] After resting and resupplying in Calicut, for three months, da Gama made the return trip to Portugal in thirteen months. This time the human cost was even greater, out of the crew of 170 who departed, only 55 returned alive. This event—discovery of a sea route from the West to the East—would forever change the course of Western and Eastern history.[106]

For Portugal, da Gama had circumvented the Asian trade monopolies of the Muslims and of the merchants from Genoa and Venice.[107] In 1502, da Gama set sail again for India and this time established a Portuguese colony at Calicut. When he returned to Portugal with his cargo of treasure, he left five ships behind which were the "the first, permanent naval force stationed by Europeans in Asiatic waters."[108] With this new outpost, the Portuguese made a concerted effort to tighten their grip on the trade route to India and exclude both Europeans and Arabs from these lucrative markets. Portugal issued a proclamation declaring themselves as "Lords of the Sea" that justified their confiscation of goods carried by all whom sailed outside of European waters without their permission. While this was a bold declaration, the Portuguese had the superior naval power to back up this inflammatory statement.[109] The building of the Indian Empire began with the first Portuguese viceroy destroying the Muslim fleet in 1509. This resolute purpose to create a monopoly resulted in the conquering of Ormuz, gateway to the Persian Gulf, in 1507, establishing Goa as the capital of the Portuguese possessions in 1510, conquering Malacca in 1511, and opening trade with Siam, the Spice Islands, and China. With these conquests, Portugal ruled the Indian Ocean and firmly established preeminence for one hundred years.[110]

This national quest, when realized, changed the world's balance of power. The wealth of the east—spices, drugs, gems, and silks—which formerly poured through Genoa and Venice on its way to Europe, was now carried by Portuguese fleets to the Iberian Peninsula. In addition, the Egyptians lost control of the pepper market and Venetian-Egyptian trade was destroyed. The Oriental riches were flowing west and the market place was no longer confined to the Mediterranean, it was open to the boundless oceans.[111]

A proverb states "success breeds complacency." Perhaps this was the reason for the downfall of the Portuguese. While the new wealth did increase the power of the King it also presented a new challenge—how to wisely manage this money. In Portugal, this new found wealth did not cover the costs of administration and war. For this reason, royal bankruptcies resulted in foreign merchant-bankers taking control of the Indies trade. Several other factors further weakened the Portuguese monopoly: the land route for Asian trade continued, albeit not as prosperous as it once was, corruption among Portuguese officials, and finally, numerous shipwrecks on the long journeys. When the Portuguese finally conceded their hegemonic position, they did so to the more economically powerful Dutch and English.[112] The Dutch took the early lead and stole the march on the spice trade. The English eventually supplanted them but the Dutch retained control of what is now Indonesia. From this time on, the balance of power in Asia shifted to northern Europe.

England: Pax Britannia

In 1588, the English took the first step in breaking the Portuguese/Spanish monopoly[113] in the East India spice trade. Sir Francis Drake, in a historic sea battle, defeated the Spanish Armada.[114] Although this success would appear to elevate England to a regional sea power, this was not the case. Both Spain and France, the then-dominant European powers, looked upon Drake's victory as merely the actions of a licensed pirate. At this time, England lacked a coordinated maritime trading strategy.[115] This is evidenced by how the English used their fleets in Drake's day. English fleets plundered in the Mediterranean and in the Americas, while in the North Sea they engaged in lawful trade.[116] The English realized they could not become a European power if they did not acquire the wealth derived from trade in a coordinated fashion. To fill this gap in a synchronized strategy, the East India Company was formed.[117]

The East India Company was formed in 1600 to exploit the trade in East and Southeast Asia and India. In 1608, the Company's first ship arrived in India and in 1612, the Company defeated the Portuguese in India.[118] With the eclipse of the Portuguese, the Company saw a massive expansion in India and established numerous trading posts as well as English communities on the east and west coasts to further secure their growing monopoly.[119] With this firm foothold, the Company developed markets in cotton and silk piece goods, indigo, saltpeter, and spices from South India. From here, the Company further expanded its trading activities to the Persian Gulf, Southeast Asia, and East Asia.[120] By the middle of the eighteenth century, the market in cotton-goods began to decline and the Company responded by opening a new market—China.[121] From China the company exported tea which developed into a growth market back home. Trade in silks and porcelain supplemented this new market.[122]

Despite these sources of wealth, from trade and tax collecting, the Company came to near collapse—due to massive military expenditures. England realized the loss of wealth and power associated with this collapse and bailed the Company out in 1773. With this national assistance came greater parliamentary oversight of the Company and India was placed under the rule of a Governor-General.[123] In the early nineteenth century, the Company began to finance the tea trade with illegal opium exports to China. This illegal trade precipitated two opium wars, which both resulted in Chinese defeats. With these victories, the English gained further trading rights thus securing their Chinese marketplace.[124]

As parliament became increasingly involved in the affairs of the Company, it ceased to be a commercial enterprise and "from 1834 it was merely a managing agency for the British government of India."[125] In 1874, the Crown completely took over operations and the Company ceased to exist. During its 274 years of existence, East India Company executed the national maritime trading strategy to perfection and as a result became the single most powerful economic force in the world. The consequences of its actions were felt through the world. The Company for example,

> created British India, caused the Boston Tea Party, founded Hong Kong and Singapore, employed Captain Kidd to combat piracy, established tea in India, held Napoleon captive, and made the fortune of Elihu Yale. Its flag inspired the Stars and Stripes, its shipyards provided the model for St. Petersburg, its administration still forms the basis of Indian Bureaucracy, and its corporate structure was the earliest example of a joint stock company. It introduced tea to the British, woolens to Japan, chintzes to America, spices to the West Indies, opium to China, porcelain to Russia, and polo to India. It had its own armies, navies, currencies, and territories

as diverse as the tiny Spice Island, Pulo Run—later exchanged for Manhattan—to the Jewel in the Crown, India itself.[126]

Much of the Company's, and later the Crown's success, testifies to the English's ability to "command the sea." They enjoyed absolute "sea supremacy" that would last from the Napoleonic era to World War I. In the age of the sail they enforced this "command" by patrolling the seas year around and thus could be stationed at the strategic points along the trading routes. With the advent of steam, England placed strategic reserves of coal around the world and denied their use to the enemy. The placement of these strategic resources allowed "the British Navy to sweep the seas of enemy warships and merchantmen alike, once the main enemy fleets had been defeated and bottled up, and to subject neutrals to search and detention or seizure."[127]

Historical Lessons Learned

At this point, one may question the relevancy of the European trading history to American space power. The European example is used to show certain ageless truths applicable to any marketplace. Four of these enduring truths are worth discussing. First, the first country to exploit a new source of wealth will enjoy the luxury of not having to displace the current leader before enjoying the lion's share of the wealth. Venice enjoyed this comfortable position for many years and defeated Genoa when directly challenged. Second, successfully exploiting a market place requires a national commitment that marries government and commercial involvement. Many times this means the government will need to assist in funding the endeavor and/or incentivize the commercial enterprise. The Portuguese realized that the pace of exploration around Africa was not at the pace needed to remain competitive or cost effective. To speed the rate of market exploration, the government incentivized sea captains by giving them a monopoly on the new trade. England's commitment to the East India Company extended to bailing out the Company when it fell on financial hard times. Third, the journey from discovery to exploitation of a new market may be long and costly. The commitment must last a sufficient amount of time to allow exploitation of the new market. In the European examples, the governments envisioned support extended over one hundred years. As a result of this long-term national policy, the states tapped into an extended source of national wealth and commensurately rose in national power. Finally, for any marketplace that is a source of wealth, there will be a contest for control of it. To lose control of this wealth means a loss of national power and therefore nations must be ready to defend it when challenged. Genoa challenged Venice directly with naval might in the Mediterranean. Portugal displayed strategic innovation by attacking Venice's monopoly with an asymmetric strategy. Rather than directly confronting Venice's fleet on it own territory, the Portuguese redefined the competition and found a new route to the eastern wealth. England established her supremacy through "command of the sea." To control any marketplace you must "command" it.

All of the above truths can be directly applied to the space marketplace. Space is a source of wealth that is waiting to be fully exploited. As such, the following are needed: government assistance and a long-term national policy. The long-term commitment to exploiting space must recognize there is a natural progression in this undertaking. While low-earth orbit (LEO) satellites currently enjoy the immediate focus, this will not always remain the case. As rocket technology advances and lowers launch costs, as orbital debris increases, and as new markets are sought out, the orbits exploited will evolve from

LEO to mid-earth orbits to geosynchronous and ultimately to the Moon and L4/L5 Lagrange points.[128] In addition to this long-term perspective, both the government and commercial business must realize the journey to wealth in and from space will be expensive. Most importantly, the control of space wealth will be challenged. The attack can come in many forms: direct attack on the orbiting space system, attack of the ground infrastructure, attack on market share through competing space systems, and attempts to gain a larger share of the global market through government subsidies. In addition, to this direct confrontation, there will be attempts to displace the U.S.'s leadership in the marketplace through indirect competition. One example of this strategic innovation (or asymmetric attack) is the assault on Iridium's market share through the development of the cellular phone market. Due to poor marketing, noncompetitive rates, expensive handsets, and weak analysis of the market place, Iridium, though technologically sound, went bankrupt.[129] The leaders in the cellular phone market are Finland and Sweden (Nokia and Ericson), hardly economic or military giants, but very successful competitors nonetheless. If the U.S. is to fully exploit space for national security as well as economic prosperity, it will require nothing short of "commanding space." All markets, including space, follow the same development cycle; exploration, investment, exploitation, and protection. Before reviewing the last two stages in the cycle it is helpful to review who had an early vision for exploring space and the national blessings that resulted.

Notes

[76] "History Part Three," 2; on-line, Internet, November 9, 2000, available from http://www.theeastindiacompany.com/history3.html and "1600-British East India Company founded," 1; on-line, Internet, November 9, 2000, available from http://www.wfu.edu/Academic-departments/History/whistory/timeline/europe/1600s/1600.htm.

Notes

[77] *Venice A Maritime Republic*, (Boston, MA: The John Hopkins University Press, 1973) 27.

[78] Ibid., 24.

[79] Ibid., 27.

[80] Ibid., 69.

[81] Ibid., 72.

[82] Ibid., 70.

[83] Ibid., 69.

[84] Ibid., 70.

[85] Ibid., 68.

[86] No medieval European navy was ever able to have full "command of the sea" of the entire Mediterranean Sea. Ibid.,67.

[87] Ibid., 68.

[88] Ibid., 23-24, 73.

[89] Ibid., 23.

[90] Ibid., 76.

[91] Ibid., 77.

[92] Ibid., 78.

[93] Ibid., 79.

[94] Ibid., 83.

[95] Ibid., 84.

[96] "Genoa-History," 2; on-line, Internet, December 8, 2000, available from http://www.eurotravelling.net/italy/genoa/genoa_history.htm.

[97] "Genoa, Italy," 2; on-line, Internet, December 8, 2000, available from http://www.comptons.com/encyclopedia/ARTICLES/0050/00727552_A.html.

[98] Daniel J. Boorstin, *The Discoverers*, (New York, NY: Random House, 1983) 159.

[99] Ibid., 160.

[100] Ibid., 157.

[101] "Portugal and Spain: Quest for Monopoly in the East," in *Civilizations under Siege The European Conquest of America*, 3; on-line, Internet, December 1, 2000, available from http://odur.let.rug.nl/~usa/E/conquest/siege13.htm.

[102] Boorstin, 168.

[103] "Portugal and Spain: Quest for Monopoly in the East."

[104] Boorstin, 173.

[105] Ibid., 175-176.

[106] Ibid., 177.

[107] Ibid., 175.

[108] Ibid., 177.

[109] "Portugal and Spain: Quest for Monopoly in the East."

[110] Boorstin, 178.

[111] Ibid.

[112] "Portugal and Spain: Quest for Monopoly in the East."

[113] At this time, the Portuguese were the dominant power in the East Indies market. This was the result of Pope Alexander intervening in 1493 to resolve the mounting

conflicts between Portugal and Spain. Under the Pope's settlement, the entire non-Christian world was divided between the two nations—Portugal was given sovereignty over the Orient and Brazil while Spain received everything else. After this agreement, the Spanish focused their energies on consolidating their position in the Americas. "Spain's Territorial Conquest of the Americas," in *Civilizations under Siege The European Conquest of America*, 2; on-line, Internet, December 1, 2000, available from http://odur.let.rug.nl/~usa/E/conquest/siege14.htm.

[114] "East India Company," 2; on-line, Internet, November 9, 2000, available from http://www.britannica.com/bcom/eb/article/6/0,5716,32316+1+31775,00.html.

[115] "History Part Two," 2; on-line, Internet, November 9, 2000, available from http://www.theeastindiacompany.com/history2.html.

[116] Fredric C. Lane, 23.

[117] "History Part Two."

[118] "East India Company."

[119] "The East India Company," 2, on-line, Internet, November 9, 2000, available from http://www.sscnet.ucla.edu/southasia/History/British/Eaco.html.

[120] "East India Company."

[121] Ibid.

[122] "History Part Two."

[123] "The East India Company."

[124] "East India Company." The two opium wars were fought from 1839-42 and from 1856-60.

[125] Ibid.

[126] "The East India Company," 3, on-line, Internet, November 9, 2000, available from http://www.theeastindiacompany.com/company.html.

[127] *Venice A Maritime Republic*, 67.

[128] "The Lagrange points for two celestial bodies in mutual revolution, such as the Earth and Moon or Earth and Sun, are the five points such that an object placed at one of them will remain there indefinite." These points require relatively small amounts of energy to maintain these orbits. Further more, these orbits are natural candidates for environmental monitoring and space manufacturing. James R. Wertz, "Orbit and Constellation Design," in *Space Mission Analysis and Design, Second Edition*, editors Wiley J. Larson and James R. Wertz, (Torrance and Dordrecht: Microcosm, Inc. and Kluwer Academic Publishers, 1993), 185.

[129] Since the bankruptcy, the new Iridium company has reduced the calling rates from $7 per minute to $1.50 per minute. In addition, the cost of the mobile handsets has dropped from $3,500 to $950. In response, to this reduction in reates, Globalstar, another global satellite-based phone service, lowered its rates to $1.49 per minute for entry-level subscribers and 89 cents per minute for high-volume users. "Iridium relaunches phone service," March 28, 2001, on-line, Internet, March 28, 2001, available from http://news.cnet.com/news/0-1004-200-5332106.html?tag=prntfr.

Chapter 7

THE QUEST

The Quest For Space

*The earth is the cradle of mankind – one cannot remain in the cradle
forever.*[130]

Konstantin Tsiolkovsky
Russian school teacher who was the first to calculate all the basic equations for
rocketry
Early 1900s

Before any nation begins a national quest, a visionary must first envisage the future.
The advocate must then articulate to national leaders why this vision should be pursued.
In other words, how will the nation profit? If the leaders are convinced this vision is a
worthy cause, national treasure is expended in pursuit of this future. With the political
support and the necessary resources, a national quest is launched. Space, as the final
frontier, is no different. An aggressive space program must first begin with the support
of the president. The successes that the U.S. enjoys today are the result of visionaries
who foresaw the promise of space, conveyed this potential to national leaders and gained
their support.

The quest for space begins with solving the problem of how to get there. Much of
this challenge was answered over a period of three centuries. Three brilliant men,

Johannes Kepler, Isaac Newton, and Konstantin Tsiolkovsky created almost all of the theory of space flight. Much of the early theory was defined not by visionaries but rather by scientific men. In 1609, Kepler, a German mathematician, developed the equations for the orbits of planets and satellites. He proved that planets moved in ellipses rather than circles. Newton followed up on this initial work and in 1687, wrote a book in which he established the laws of force, motion, and gravitation. He was able to show that the force of gravity was the reason why planets traveled in ellipses. While these men explained the celestial motions of planets, they did not expound on how to get into space. This challenge was resolved in 1903 by Tsiolkovsky a Russian schoolteacher. He calculated all of the basic equations for rocketry and what makes his work even more significant is that he did this without ever launching a rocket. Even with his lack of operational experience, he accurately anticipated many of the problems associated with a rocket launch. He determined that liquid fuel rockets—best fueled by oxygen and hydrogen— were the optimal means to reach space. He also put forth that multiple stage rockets were necessary. What is most interesting to note about Tsiolkovsky is where he received much of this inspiration for his breakthrough. He was an extensive reader who read the book entitled *From the Earth to the Moon* by Jules Verne. From these readings, he determined that space travel was not only possible but it was man's destiny and rockets were the means to achieve this end.[131]

Jules Verne: Visionary Patriarch of Space

The French author Jules Verne is most often remembered for his adventure novels, which thrilled children. Who can forget Captain Nemo fighting the giant squid in *Twenty Thousand Leagues Under the Sea* or all the exotic places visited by Phineas Fogg and his servant in *Around the World in 80 Days*? What many people fail to realize is that Jules Verne's writing was meticulously grounded in fact. As such, Verne raised his writing style of scientific verisimilitude to a fine art.[132] The common people were not the only ones to appreciate this style of writing but also scientists and engineers. Within the scientific community, many space pioneers were inspired to greatness because of his writings. Konstantin Tsiolkovshi was one the first space pioneers to read Verne's novels and he calculated the basic equations of rocketry in 1903. Robert Goddard, an American who is called "the father of modern rocketry," was heavily influenced by Verne's writings and also developed the theory of rocketry independent of Tsiolkovshi's work. Hermann Oberth, a German engineer, read Verne's space novel at age eleven and went on to also develop the principles of rocketry, independent of Tsiolkovshi and Goddard.[133] Each of these men, from all corners of the globe, was aggressively provoked to make Verne's scientific verisimilitude into a reality. Verne's inspiration did not stop with these men. Yuri Gagarin, the first human to fly in space, and Neil Armstrong, the first man to walk on the Moon, were also moved by Verne's writings to greatness.[134]

Two Verne books that served as a catalyst for many space breakthroughs were *From the Earth to the Moon* and *Around the Moon*. In these two prophetic novels, Verne chose a launch site not far from the present day Cape Canaveral, accurately calculated the escape velocity needed to overcome the Earth's gravitation, correctly described the effects of weightlessness, and pictured the fiery reentry and splashdown in the Pacific at a site not three miles from where Apollo 11 landed. With these scientific insights, it should not be surprising that Verne's calculated answers are very similar to the modern astronautical solutions.[135] These fictional novels, with their scientific foundation, served as the jumping off point for three men who would make space flight a fact. The first two men—Tsiolkovshi and Oberth—made rockets a reality, while the third man, Wernher Von Braun, made the landing on the Moon a reality.

Wernher von Braun: German-American Prophet

Wernher von Braun was so inspired by the reading of Verne's works that he flourished as one of the world's foremost proponents of space exploration from the 1930s all the way to the 1970s. During the 1950's, he took on a "Billy Mitchell" role as the most enthusiastic spokesman in the United States for space travel.[136] Dr. von Braun however, was not all talk; his commitment to "go where no man has gone before" led to him to become one of the world's preeminent rocket engineers.[137]

In 1912, Wernher von Braun was born in Wirsitz, Germany. As a youth, he was enamoured with the possibilities of space flight that he read about in Verne's novels and this interest would forever change his destiny as well as the world's future. In the early thirties, he joined the Germany army to build ballistic missiles. By 1934, he earned a Ph.D. in aerospace engineering and he continued his work on rockets. During World War II, he was one of the chief engineers on the then secret V-2 rocket. The V-2 was a liquid propelled missile, 46 feet in length, weighed 27,000 pounds, flew in excess of 3,500 miles per hour, and delivered a 2,200-pound warhead on a target 500 miles away.[138] Dr. von Braun was not only an engineer; he was also a visionary. In the last year of the War, the SS and Gestapo arrested him for crimes against the state. His crime? He persisted in talking about building bigger rockets, which would orbit the earth and go on to the Moon. Nazi leadership felt this frivolous dreaming took his concentration away from his primary purpose of building bigger bombs. Upon his release, Dr. von Braun immediately began planning his escape from Germany. He eventually surrendered to the Americans, along with 500 from his staff. The Americans recognized the value of these engineers and immediately went to the secret V-2 production sites. From these sites, the Americans shipped over 300 train carloads of V-2 spare parts.[139] After the War, this war treasure served to jump-start the America ballistic missile program.

The war in Europe was over but the first battle of the Cold War was about to be played out. Soon after the American and Soviet liberators converged in Germany, the competition was on for the V-2 rocket engineers. In June 1945, von Braun and 126 other V-2 staffers were brought to America as the result of the success of "Operation Paperclip." It was one of the most important operations of WW II and allowed the U.S. to capture the best of the Nazi rocket program. He and his men were brought to Ft Bliss, Texas to begin the process of rebuilding and launching the V-2s as well as training military, industry, and university personnel on the intricacies of rocketry.[140] With his engineering prowess proven, Dr. von Braun and his team were transferred to Huntsville, Alabama where he would live for the next twenty years. He began work on the Army's Redstone rocket and this led to the Jupiter-C rocket, which launched the first U.S. satellite into space on January 31, 1958.[141]

With these small successes, Dr. von Braun returned to stating his dreams in public. In 1952, he published his concept of a space station in Collier's magazine. During this time he also began working with Disney studios as a technical director for three films on space exploration. After these films, he continued his work with Disney in the hopes that Disney's involvement would increase and stimulate the public awareness of space. Dr. von Braun did his part to further manned space flight as he was at the center of the

Mercury program. In 1960, Dr. von Braun became the first director of NASA's Marshall Space Flight Center, a position he would hold for ten years.[142] From here, he returned to his childhood dreams of going to the Moon.

Dr. von Braun's first major program at the Marshall Center was nothing short of his dreams—develop a rocket capable of sending an astronaut to the Moon.[143] Since this was his destiny, he put his heart and soul into the Saturn V rocket program. His engineering expertise was reflected in the fact that the Saturn rockets were the only series that worked perfectly on every launch—not a one blew up on the pad.[144] On 16 July 1969, Dr. von Braun's and a nation's dream was fulfilled with the landing of the Apollo 11 crew on the Moon. Over the course of the Apollo program, a total of six teams would travel to the Moon before the program was terminated in 1972. This however, was not the end of Dr. von Braun's dreams. In 1973, a Saturn 1B rocket, also developed under his leadership, launched Skylab the world's first space station. The final use of Dr. von Braun's Saturn rockets was the historic Apollo-Soyuz linkup in 1975.[145]

In June 1977, Dr. von Braun died from cancer with a legacy in space unparalleled by modern man. Here was a man who not only followed Jules Verne vision to reach the Moon but also labored to make it a reality. His technical skills along with the essential national support enabled America to win the space race. America had begun its quest to "command space." However, scientific breakthroughs alone will not lead to full command of space. Commercialization of space is needed to reap the potential wealth from space.

Arthur C. Clark: English Prophet

Just mention the name, Arthur C. Clark, and millions of people immediately associate this name with the book and movie *2001: A Space Odyssey*. He is one of the most celebrated science fiction writers with over sixty books published, over 50 million copies in print, and winner of all major awards in this field of writing. In recognition of his writing prowess, the Science Fiction Writers of America named him Grand Master in 1985. Numerous honors preceded this lifetime achievement award: the Hugo award, twice; the Nebula award, three times; and the John W. Campbell Award, for best new writer.[146] In addition to *2001: A Space Odyssey*, his other best sellers include: *Childhood's End, 2010: Odyssey Two, 2061: Odyssey Three, 3001: The Final Odyssey, Rama II, The Garden of Rama*, and *Rama Revealed*.[147] Without a doubt the world will remember Clarke as one of the great science fiction writers of all time.

Perhaps the key to Clarke's writing success lies in the fact that he, like Jules Verne, possessed a technical grounding. In World War II, he served as a Royal Air Force officer in charge of the first radar talk-down equipment, used by airmen for ground controlled approaches. Following the war, he graduated with first class honors in Physics and Mathematics from King's College in London.[148] This technical training and education permitted him to envision the future, some of which he has seen come to pass.

In 1945, Clarke published a technical paper entitled, "Extra Terrestrial Relays, Can Rocket Stations Give World-wide Radio Coverage?" in which he laid down the principle of satellite communications from satellites in geostationary orbits. In this paper, he accurately showed the advantages of communication satellites over relay stations, in the areas of cost, reliability, and coverage. He calculated the rocket velocity required to reach the geostationary orbit as well as the power required to broadcast. While he admitted that his proposal might appear "too far fetched to be taken seriously," he denounced this skepticism as "unreasonable."[149] He pointed out that his proposal was just a natural extension of the current state of the art developments in rocketry. In this paper, he also recorded that the Germans, with the recent success of the V-2 rocket, were considering a similar satellite communications project.[150] Eighteen years later and only five years after Sputnik was launched, America won another battle in the race to command space when it successfully deployed the world's first geostationary communication satellite.[151] This was only possible because the U.S. acted on the written promises of this visionary. He is recognized around the world for inventing geostationary communication satellites and has received numerous honors for this achievement. In addition, the International Astronomical Union named this unique orbit "The Clarke Orbit."[152]

Clarke's vision of the future did not stop with geostationary communication satellites. In 1954, he wrote to Dr. Harry Wexler, Chief of the Scientific Services Division, U.S. Weather Bureau, about the use of satellites for weather forecasting. Based on this vision, a new branch of meteorology was created and "Dr. Wexler became the driving force in using rockets and satellites for meteorological research and operations."[153] Six years later, this vision also became a reality with the launching of TIROS, which was designed to collect meteorological data.[154] America achieved another milestone in commanding space and thus improved its ability to collect global information. Today anyone who watches the weather report on television profits from this foresight by Clarke. With better weather forecasting, man is better able to anticipate and plan accordingly rather than reacting in an unprepared manner.

Clark's vision of satellite communications is one that endures to this day and the future holds increased realization of this promise. His vision of communication satellites continues to grow and has developed into the largest commercial market in space.[155] As a result of the United States acting on this vision, it was able to take the early lead in this information market and currently remains the dominant player in the global satellite communications market. With the dominant position in the marketplace, the U.S. increases its command of space and thus enjoys a larger share of the wealth derived from information.

It is significant to note that just as the European government's financed and spearheaded the drive to open new markets in the second millennium, the same holds true for communication satellites as well as space systems in general. The government must take the lead in opening access to these potential markets and then corporate America will follow. The U.S. did not become the dominant market shareholder thorough government research and projects alone. It took the investment of American business to fully exploit this marketplace. To remain competitive in the space sector, business must continue to demonstrate strategic innovation in maintaining current markets and creating new ones. Both government and corporate America must work together if this country is to fully harvest the wealth and strategic security from space. Failure to follow this guidance will result in the nation losing command of space.

A Current Space Perspective

In the European quest for wealth by sea power, we saw that it took hundreds of years to learn and know the cycle of knowledge, exploitation, investment, consumption and protection. When nation's failed to respect the importance of one of these elements, they lost the market lead and waned in global power. For America, we have been learning and growing in knowledge for about 400 years and as a result we remain the only superpower in the world. In space, we accelerated our learning and duplicated this same success in about 40 years. In the past, our space vision was on exploration and knowledge. However, the current vision has advanced to investment and consumption. The one element that is missing in the vision is protection of the space marketplace. While we learned and appreciated this concept terrestrially, we did not apply it to space. So far, the nation is fortunate it has not suffered a major attack on its space architecture—a Space Pearl Harbor.

The Global Positioning System is but one space system that demonstrates the current vision of investment and consumption. American business is applying strategic innovation to create and open new GPS markets. As a result of this focus, the nation benefits from a space industry that is measured in the hundreds of billion dollars. While application of the current vision certainly amplifies our nation's prosperity and security, these two vital interests are not secure. As a result of a lack of protection, the nation's space infrastructure and marketplace are at risk. The international competition is slowly chipping away at the nation's marketshare as well as security derived from these systems. Before addressing the protection issue, it is helpful to first review the prosperity derived from space. The GPS is but one example of the promise in space and is used as a representative case study.

Notes

[130]Randy Culp, "History of Space Travel," October 27, 1998, 4; on-line, Internet, November 9, 2000, available from http://www.execpc.com/~culp/space/history.html.

[131] Ibid.

[132] Arthur B. Evans and Ron Miller, "Jules Verne, Misunderstood Visionary," April 1997, 11; on-line, Internet, November 9, 2000, available from http://www.sciam.com/0497issue/0497evans.html.

[133] Culp.

[134] Arthur B. Evans and Ron Miller.

[135] Ibid.

[136] "Wernher von Braun (1912-1977)," August 25, 1997, 2; on-line, Internet, October 24, 2000, available from http://www.hq.nasa.gov/office/pao/History/sputnik/braun.html.

[137] "Wernher Von Braun," April 3, 2000, 1; on-line, Internet, October 24, 2000, available from http://www.liftoff.msfc.nasa.gov/academy/history/vonBraun/vonBraun.html.

[138] "Wernher von Braun (1912-1977)."

[139] "Von Braun: Germany," April 3, 2000, 2; on-line, Internet, October 24, 2000, available from http://www.liftoff.msfc.nasa.gov/academy/history/vonBraun/germany.html.

[140] "Von Braun: Moving to the U.S.," April 3, 2000, 2; on-line, Internet, October 24, 2000, available from http://www.liftoff.msfc.nasa.gov/academy/history/vonBraun/moving.html.

[141] "Von Braun: The Beginning of the Space Age," April 3, 2000, 2; on-line, Internet, October 24, 2000, available from http://www.liftoff.msfc.nasa.gov/academy/history/vonBraun/SpaceAge.html.

[142] Ibid.

[143] "Von Braun: The Space Age Continues," April 3, 2000, 2; on-line, Internet, October 24, 2000, available from http://www.liftoff.msfc.nasa.gov/academy/history/vonBraun/spaceage2.html.

[144] Randy Culp.

[145] Von Braun: The Space Age Continues."

[146] "Arthur C. Clarke Unauthorized Homepage," July 18, 2000, 2; on-line, Internet, December 14, 2000, available from http://www.lsi.usp.br/~rbianchi/clrake/ and "The Hugo Award," September 2, 2000, 1; on-line, Internet, January 10, 2001, available from http://worldcon.org/hugos.html.

[147] "Arthur C. Clarke Unauthorized Homepage."

[148] "Arthur C. Clarke Biography," 5; on-line, Internet, December 14, 2000, available from http://www.lsi.usp.br/~rbianchi/clarke/ACC.Biography.html.

[149] Satellites in the geostationary orbit, approximately 36,000 kilometers in altitude, orbit once around the Earth in one day. For this reason, the satellite appears to remain fixed in the sky since it is moving at the same rate as the Earth's rotation. From this

vantagepoint, a satellite is able to "see" approximately one third of the Earth's surface. This coverage is the area in which satellite communications can be conducted by one satellite. A three-ball satellite constellation, equally spaced 120 degrees apart in this orbit, will provide near-total Earth coverage. "Arthur C. Clarke Extra Terrestrial Relays," February 28, 1996, 6; on-line, Internet, December 14, 2000, available from http://www.lsi.usp.br/~rbianchi/clarke/ACC.ETRelaysFull.html.

[150] The Germans predicted satellite communication would be possible in fifty to one hundred years. Ibid.

[151] The first geostationary satellite was launched on July 26, 1963 and was named Syncom 2. This launch was preceded by earlier successes with satellite communication. The first satellite communication experiment was the U.S.'s Project SCORE launched on December 18, 1958. "Satellite Communication," 4; on-line, Internet, January 17, 2001, available   from http://www.britannica.com/bcom/eb/article/1/0,5716,67541+2+65845,00.html.

[152] "Arthur C. Clarke Biography."

[153] Ibid.

[154] TIROS—Television Infrared Operational System—was operated by the National Oceanic and Atmospheric Administration (NOAA). "About NCDC's Satellite Resources," 11; on-line, Internet, January 17, 2001, available from http://www.ncdc.noaa.gov/ol/satellite/satelliteresourcesabout.html.

[155] "ESA-Satellite Applications – Telecommunications," 4; on-line, Internet, January 19,   2001,   available   from http://www.esa.int/export/esaSA/GGGATV50NDC_telecom_0.html.

Chapter 8

THE PROMISE

GPS: A Case Study in Success

The GPS continues to mature into a worldwide dual-use positioning, navigation, and timing resource. ... Worldwide civil applications of GPS continue to expand, with new and innovative uses of GPS appearing continuously.[156]

William S. Cohen
Secretary of Defense
2000 Annual Report to the President

The development and exploitation of Global Positioning System (GPS) illustrates the same principles learned by the Europeans in developing and exploiting the maritime trade routes. The knowledge gained from the Transit satellite navigation system was used to begin exploration for a new replacement. After investment by the government, a GPS constellation was put in place, and consumption began by the government and the private sector. As consumption increased, the private sector invested their own monies and created new markets. As a result, consumption increased and new competitors entered to challenge the American market. All of this development is covered in greater detail in the following paragraphs.

Original Purpose

Today the use of the GPS is just as common among the civilian populace as in the military. It is interesting to note that the original design never envisioned this dual use. According to the GPS Joint Program Office, this space system was developed exclusively as a military system and was never intended for the commercial sector.[157] The Navy's ballistic missile submarines were one of the first military users of GPS. These same weapons systems were also the impetus for the United States' first satellite navigation network, Transit, begun in the early 1960s. To permit these systems to accurately target ballistic missiles in Soviet silos, it was necessary to have precise location data. Transit initially provided what now is provided by the GPS.[158]

In 1978 the USAF launched the first Block I series GPS satellite with another nine launched through 1988. From 1989 to 1993, twenty-three Block II satellites were launched and the launch of the twenty-fourth satellite in 1994 completed the satellite constellation.[159] The GPS constellation is arranged in six orbital planes with four satellites, equally spaced at 60 degrees, and inclined at about 55 degrees with respect to the equatorial plane. This arrangement provides the user with five to eight visible satellites from any point on the earth.[160] With three satellites, a GPS receiver can determine accurate latitude and longitude information and with a fourth satellite, precise altitude information can also be determined. When more satellites are in view, the accuracy of this information increases. From the beginning, military users accessed the Precise Code (P-code) which allowed 10-16 meter accuracy. Civilians did not enjoy this same level of accuracy. They only had access to the Coarse/Acquisition (C/A) code, which provides approximately 30-meter accuracy. In mid-1990 the C/A code was encrypted under Selective Availability and its accuracy degraded to 100 meters.[161] The commercial market, through the engineering community, responded to this degradation with the creation of differential GPS. With this system, GPS accuracy can be improved to less than one meter.[162] The U.S. Government was aware of this reality and turned off Selective Availability in May 2000.[163] As the GPS constellation matured, so the military's use of GPS also developed.

DESERT STORM provided a watershed event for advancing the use of GPS within the military. At the beginning of this conflict, only 1,000 portable commercial receivers were supplied to the troops. Due to their initial success, over 12,000 commercial receivers were in use by the end of the conflict.[164] One of the earliest combat successes occurred on the first night of the air campaign. According to the Pentagon's final report of the Gulf War, GPS enabled the successful helicopter raid on the Iraqi early-warning radar network.[165] This one success opened the door for the rest of the air armada to proceed to their bombing targets. Another application seen in the desert was the use of small GPS receivers on munitions. If the location of the target was known, this information could be encoded into the targeting mechanism and thereby create smart munitions out of dumb ones. GPS was also successfully applied to ground operations. GPS allowed the Army to create a new formation for a heavy brigade to maintain positive command and control in the Desert. The *wedge* formation allowed fluid movement over vast distances during combat. According to Col. House, Commander of the 2[d] Brigade, 1st Calvary Division, the brigade wedge was the "most important command and control asset and combat multiplier of the war for 2[d] Brigade."[166] The Navy used GPS technology on their ships for rendezvous and minesweeping as well as aircraft operations.[167] Across the services, the GPS constellation is indispensable to any military operation, whether in combat operations or peacetime engagement.

The commercial market saw this military space system as a golden opportunity to win the war for market share. No other satellite system allows free access to a $17-billion, on-orbit system along with no payment toward the $500 million annual operational costs. In addition to this free access, GPS vendors are confident the military will maintain the system even in the event of damage by solar flares, meteor showers, or other acts of God. The final enticement for industry was that there were no monthly charges for the user.[168] With these incentives, a whole new market was created, one that was never envisioned in the beginning of GPS and one that has many more users than the military.[169]

Commercial Applications

Two technology developments are propelling the GPS commercial market. The first advancement is differential GPS, which allowed accuracy to a few feet rather than a hundred feet. The second improvement is the shrinking price of GPS receiver chips to about ten dollars. This breakthrough allowed industry to create a product that was affordable to the average consumer.[170] These two advances allowed the market to expand beyond the traditional uses for GPS navigation: surveying and mapping, marine navigation and aviation.[171]

One the largest markets for GPS receivers is car navigation including in-vehicle communication, in-vehicle navigation, electronic toll collection, automatic vehicle identification, automatic vehicle location, and collision avoidance. In 1988, this growing market surpassed the $1 billion mark and it is expected to grow to over $18 billion annually by 2003.[172] In 1998, Hertz, the world's largest car rental company, installed 50,000 GPS receivers in their cars to provide vehicle navigation and driver information.[173] In this same year, GM had over 14,000 autos equipped with the OnStar system, which provides "cellular communications, mayday support, navigation and point of interest directions."[174] It is surprising to note that the U.S. is not the global leader in exploiting this application of GPS. In fact, the lucrative U.S. market remains relatively untapped. The Japanese lead the way and in 1997 they already had close to one million cars equipped with these navigation systems.[175] As prices continue to fall, the market will continue to increase in size and profitability.

The second market that is just beginning to take off, thanks to federal regulation, is the cellular phone market. The Federal Communications Commission has mandated that by October 2001; all cellular/PCS networks will incorporate an automatic caller location feature when calling 911. This market amounts to hundreds of millions of phones over the next four years and is expected to dominate more than 20 percent of the global market in 2005.[176]

The third largest market is Vehicle/Freight tracking. Tracking can begin at the warehouses where goods are loaded onto the transportation vehicle. As the vehicle leaves the warehouse, a GPS transceiver will emit location data to the headquarters and thereby improve the flow of goods and decrease the cost of control tracking.[177] Already it is estimated that 20 percent of the commercial trucking fleet is equipped with GPS receivers for location tracking.[178] Local governments are also managing their transportation systems using this same technology. A Pennsylvania community uses GPS-aided dispatch system to manage "a fleet of 1,627 buses, light rail, and maintenance and supervisory vehicles."[179] The quantity of vehicle/freight tracking will only increase as the costs continue to decline and as this system is also installed on railcars and maritime cargo ships.

The market does not stop with these three major categories. As different business sectors are educated on the application of GPS, additional markets are emerging. One famous use of GPS was in the construction of the "Chunnel" under the English Channel. Both the English and French construction crews used GPS receivers to keep the tunnel straight thus ensuring they met squarely in the middle. Had the crews not used GPS, there was a good chance the Chunnel would have been crooked. Another market that is expanding rapidly is emergency services. Many police, fire and ambulance units are using GPS to determine the vehicle closest to the emergency, "enabling the quickest possible response in life-or-death situations."[180]

Continued improvements in precision agriculture, mentioned earlier, are another market that is emerging. To further automate agriculture production, GPS-based irrigation now brings a tele-robotic capability to provide precise and efficient irrigation. This system assures "continual adjustment of speed and steering critical for precise, full-field irrigation."[181] Another agriculture application of GPS is the control of farm tractors. With GPS technology, these tractors can autonomously cross a field, while holding their position to plus or minus one inch.[182] This same concept also allows farming combines to harvest the crops on autopilot.[183] Environmentalists and scientists also use GPS for tracking purposes. Threatened animal species can be fitted with tiny GPS transceivers to determine population distribution patterns. GPS-equipped balloons are monitoring the ozone loss over the polar regions and air pollution is also being monitored with GPS

70

receivers. Finally, buoys are used to track oil spills by transmitting GPS-derived location data.[184]

Several novel uses of GPS have created niche markets. The golfing industry is coming into the 21st century with the use of electronic golf carts that incorporate GPS technology. These new carts feature "a hole and green overview, exact distancing, electronic score-keeping, food and beverage ordering, pro tips and two-way communications."[185] Golfing will never be the same. Lastly, the law enforcement community is also benefiting from GPS location information. Industry has created ankle bracelets that transmit wireless location data back to a surveillance center. This solution provides law enforcement officers with a better method for tracking offenders who are on probation or parole.[186] Another application for combating crime is the combination of automatic teller machines (ATM) and GPS trackers. Since ATMs typically carry large amounts of money and are increasingly becoming portable—some as little as 200 pounds—they are prime targets for thieves. One ATM company has developed a solution to this problem. When one of these GPS-equipped ATMs are compromised, the tracker notifies a security monitoring office with the location, speed and direction of travel. The local authorities are then contacted and directed to the ATM before the thieves are able to break into it.[187]

These examples are by no means representative of the whole GPS market but are rather given to show the diversity of applications. What is even more noteworthy is that market growth shows no sign of slowing or decreasing in size.

Continued Growth Market

The commercial GPS industry is a multi-billion business that is not confined to the U.S. In 1997, the domestic share of this global market was $1 billion.[188] Since then, the global GPS market has grown to its present market size of $9 billion.[189] The Frost & Sullivan research firm forecasts that this market will continue to grow at a steady 20 percent for the next few years.[190] Other analysts forecast a smaller market size of $14 billion by 2005[191] while others predict a larger market of $20 billion as soon as 2002.[192] While no one can accurately predict the future, it is obvious the GPS applications market will continue to experience robust growth.

Just because the U.S. created the GPS system does not guarantee it will continue to reap the financial rewards of being the first on orbit—first to market. The rest of the world sees this economic frontier and is aggressively seeking to increase their market share. Currently, the U.S. dominates the commercial GPS market with a 65 percent share. However, five years from now it is estimated that 50 percent of GPS equipment will be produced outside of the U.S.[193] In addition to increasing market share, several countries are raising financial support to create alternative space navigation systems.

The DOD management of GPS appears to be the root motivation for these rival countries. They want guaranteed critical location, navigation and timing information and at the same time not be subject to the whims of the U.S. government. These concerns peaked a few years ago when several countries of the International Telecommunications Union attempted to play financial hardball. Forty-seven countries, from Europe and Asia, were in agreement to reserve a portion of the radio spectrum already in use by GPS and use it for European-based cellular communications. Had this been allowed, the

European systems would have jammed the GPS signal. This hostile action was only averted by the direct intervention of NATO commander Wesley Clark. General Clark "called 10 Downing Street and said 'Look, we're carrying your water in Iraq and Bosnia. Stop messing around with us.'"[194] This event points out that the U.S. could lose its command of space unless they are vigilant in defending and expanding American utilization of it.

The Russian Glonass constellation and the European Union's Galileo system pose the two most serious challenges. Glonass is already on orbit although it is not fully functional. The complete system requires 24 satellites and currently, only 14 on are on orbit and out of these only nine are operational. With their collapsing economy, the Russians realize they will not be able to "go it alone" and so have invited the Chinese to help with financing some of the Glonass satellites. So far the Chinese have only showed an interest in acquiring Glonass terminals but high level talks, at the President and Prime Minister level, continue on the topic of Glonass financing.[195] Galileo is still in development, but quickly gaining financial support to make this concept a reality. In 1998, the European Union established a GPS-like group to map out the strategy for acquiring such a system. The result was a two phased approach. Phase one entailed the development of a space-based augmentation system to GPS and Glonass by 2002. Phase two consisted of an alternative GPS constellation called Galileo.[196] This $2.7 billion project is scheduled to begin operations in 2005 and become fully operational three years later.[197] The rest of the world is taking this alternative GPS system seriously and offering help. In June 2000, Ukraine signed on with the European Union to cooperate in the creation of this all-European, spaced-based navigation system.[198] In October 2000,

Russia began negotiations with the European Union to assist them in launching their navigation satellites.[199] In Jan 2001, the Italian Parliament approved $291 million funding toward the project.[200] All of these developments will further chip away at the U.S.'s market share unless the nation is proactive in responding to this challenge.

A third challenge that is just beginning to emerge is the Chinese Beidou Navigation System. On 31 October 2000, the Chinese launched the first of four indigenous navigation satellites. This system is envisioned to be an all-weather, regional navigation system that provides 24-hour service to highway, rail, and marine transportation.[201] With this system in place, Chinese reliance on GPS is at best reduced and at worst, totally eliminated. Only time will tell how the successful the Chinese will be in this endeavor.

Fortunately, the U.S. commercial industry is aware of these challenges and at least one company is responding. Lockheed Martin is developing a space and terrestrial-based augmentation system for air traffic navigation. This $1.1 billion project[202] will initially provide service to North, Central, and South American and eventually, the service could be seamlessly expanded into a global system as other countries commit to this service.[203] To maintain and advance its market share, industry must be aggressive in launching new information systems that will keep it competitive in global information commerce. The future development of GPS boundless and is only limited by one's imagination. As technology evolves, new applications are sure to follow. GPS satellites are like beacons in the sky that will guide commercial exploitation well into the 21st century."[204]

For continued prosperity in this new century, the nation, as a whole, must advance the GPS system as well as all other satellite systems. However, when any nation expands it marketshare, it will be challenged. If the challenge is not met, the result is usually a loss of marketshare such that the end is worse than the beginning. The same principle holds true for space. Although the U.S. is the recognized leader in space, it is continuing to lose marketshare due to little protection of the marketplace. This nation must protect and defend its investment in space. In addition, America must develop new markets in space through strategic innovation. Failure to take the initiative in these two areas will result in the nation losing command of space.

Notes

[156] William S. Cohen, Secretary of Defense, *Annual Report to the President and the Congress*, 21; on-line, Internet, November 30, 2000, available from http://www.dtic.mil/execsec/adr2000/chap8.html.

[157] Claire Tristram, "Has GPS Lost Its Way?," 8; on-line, Internet, November 9, 2000, available from http://www.techreview.com/articles/july99/tristram.htm.

[158] Christina Lindborg, "Navigation," March 9, 1997, 10; on-line, Internet, November 17, 2000, available from http://www.fas.org/spp/military/program/nav/overview/htm and Andrew P. Madden, "Lost in Space," April 1997, 7; on-line, Internet, November 9, 2000, available from http://www.redherring.com/mag/issue41/space.html.

[159] "Satellites in Space," Aerospace Corporation GPS Primer, March 29, 1999, 1; on-line, Internet, November 30, 2000, available from http://www.aero.org/publications/GPSPRIMER/

[160] Peter H. Dana, "Global Positioning System Overview," May 1, 2000, 12; on-line, Internet, available from http://www.colorado.edu/geography/gcraft/notes/gps/gps.html.

[161] Christina Lindborg.

[162] "GPS Elements," Aerospace Corporation GPS Primer, March 29, 1999, 1; on-line, Internet, November 30, 2000, available from http://www.aero.org/publications/GPSPRIMER/

[163] Peter H. Dana.

[164] Sir Peter Anson and Dennis Cummings, "The First Space War: The Contribution of Satellite to the Gulf War," in *The First Information War*, ed Alan D. Campen, (Fairfax, VA: AFCEA International Press, 1992), 127.

[165] Alvin Toffler and Heidi Toffler, *War and Anti-War: Survival at the Dawn of the Twenty-First Century*, (Boston, MA: Little, Brown and Company, 1993), 3.

[166] Randolph W. House and Gregory L. Johnson, "C2 in a Heavy Brigade," in *The First Information War*, ed Alan D. Campen, (Fairfax, VA: AFCEA International Press, 1992), 101-102, 106.

[167] "Military Uses for GPS," Aerospace Corporation GPS Primer, March 29, 1999, 1; on-line, Internet, November 30, 2000, available from http://www.aero.org/publications/GPSPRIMER/

Notes

[168] Claire Tristram, "Has GPS Lost Its Way?," July/August 1999, 8; on-line, Internet, November 9, 2000, available from http://www.techreview.com/articles/july99/tristram.htm.

[169] Andrew P. Madden.

[170] Claire Tristram.

[171] Andrew P. Madden.

[172] "Car Navigation a Billion Dollar Market Says Allied," August 20, 1998, 2; on-line Internet, November 30, 2000, available from http://www.spacedaily.com/news/gps-98l.html.

[173] "Orbital to Outfit 50,000 Hertz Cars With GPS," December 15, 1998, 3; on-line, Internet, November 9, 200, available from http://www.spacedaily.com/news/orbsci-98q.html.

[174] "Car Navigation a Billion Dollar Market Says Allied."

[175] Andrew P. Madden. In mid-1997, the Japanese market for GPS receivers on autos was already over $1.5 billion in size.

[176] "News GPS Market Worth $14 Billion by 2005," 2; on-line, Internet, November 9, 2000, available from http://www.itsa.org/85256201003EFA03/0/6508EF390D4258FD852567770052BFAF?Open and Carrie Kirby, "New Technology Can Pinpoint Cell-Phone User's Locations Police see benefit in emergencies—watchdogs fear erosion of privacy," October 23, 2000, 5; on-line, Internet, October 25, 2000, available from http://www.sfgate.com/cbi-bin/article.cgi?file=/chronicle/article/2000/1.../BU77211.DTL&type=tech_articl.

[177] Ibid.

[178] "Car Navigation a Billion Dollar Market Says Allied."

[179] "Pennsylvania Keeps to the Track With Orbital," November 30, 1999, 3; on-line, Internet, November 30, 2000, available from http://www.spacedaily.com/news/orbtrac-00a.html.

[180] "GPS Uses in Everyday Life," Aerospace Corporation GPS Primer, March 29, 1999, 1; on-line, Internet, November 30, 2000, available from http://www.aero.org/publications/GPSPRIMER/

[181] "GPS Bringing Robotics To The Farm," August 24, 1999, 3; on-line, Internet, November 9, 2000, available from http://www.spacedaily.com/news/gps-99p.html.

[182] Andrew Madden.

[183] "Trimble Brings GPS Precision to Agriculture," GPS Update, February 8, 2000, on-line, Internet, November 9, 2000, available from http://www.spacedaily.com/gps.html.

[184] "GPS Uses in Everyday Life."

[185] "ParView scores with GPS for golf carts, November 27, 1998, 1; on-line, Internet, November 16, 2000, available from http://www.bizjournals.com/tampabay/stories/1998/11/23/daily10.html?t=printable.

[186] "GPS Creates a Global Jail," April 8, 1998, 3; on-line, Internet, November 9, 2000, available from http://www.spacedaily.com/news/gps-98e.ht//ml.

[187] "GPS Tracks ATM Bandits," August 20, 1998, 3; on-line, Internet, November 9, 2000, available from http://www/spacedaily.com/news/gps-98k.html.

[188] Claire Tristram.

Notes

[189] Lieutenant General Donald G. Cook, "Royal United Services Institute for Defense Studies Military Utility of Space Conference Keynote Address," Whitehall, London, September 8, 1999, 6; on-line, Internet, November 28, 2000, available from http://www.spacecom.af.mil/hqafspc/library/speeches/royal_inst.htm.

[190] Claire Tristram.

[191] "GPS 2005 Global Opportunities in Satellite Navigation Technologies," 7; on-line Internet, November 9, 2000, available from http://www.dri.co.jp/ABI/gps99.htm.

[192] Naser El-Sheimy, "Integrated Systems and their Impact on the Future of Positioning, Navigation, and Mapping Applications," Quo Vadis – International Conference, May 21-26, 2000, 10; on-line, Internet, November 9, 2000, available from http://www.ddl.org/figtree/pub/proceedings/prague-final-papers/el-sheimy.htm.

[193] "News GPS Market Worth $14 Billion by 2005."

[194] Claire Tristram. It is significant those within these 47 countries were some of our closest allies: Britain, Germany, France, Italy, Spain, Japan, Korea, Australia, New Zealand, Brazil and Mexico. Before General Clark's intervention, we only have six votes in our favor for protecting the portion of the spectrum used by GPS.

[195] "China Could Help Fund Russian GPS Network," July 25, 2000, 2; on-line, Internet, November 30, 2000, available from http://www.spacedaily.com/news/gps-00h.html.

[196] "Europe Establishes GPS Group," June 20, 1998, 3; on-line, Internet, November 9, 2000, available from http://www.spacedaily/news/euro-gps-98a.html.

[197] "Europe to Decide on GPS Challenge," December 7, 1999, 3; on-line, Internet, November 9, 2000, available from http://www.spacedaily.com/news/galileo-ps-99b.html.

[198] "Ukraine Planning to Join European GPS Program," June 30, 2000, 2; on-line, Internet, November 30, 2000, available from http://www.spacedaily.com/news/gps-euro-00c.html.

[199] "Russia Eyes Role in Euro Net," October 30, 2000, 3; on-line, Internet, November 1, 2000, available from http://www.spacer.com/news/gps-euro-00d.html.

[200] Major Jeff Witko and Major Jose Caussade, "GPS for Air and Space Power," February 12, 2001, No. 239.

[201] "China Puts 1st Navigation Positioning Satellite into Orbit," October 31, 2000, 3; on-line, Internet, November 1, 2000, available from http://www.geocities.com/CapeCanaveral/Launchpad/1921/news.htm.

[202] "Lockheed Martin forms GPS company (Flight International)," March 28, 2000, 1; on-line, Internet, November 30, 2000, available from http://www.industry.esa.int/CGForum/get/indust02/13.html.

[203] "LockMart Eyes Own GPS," June 28, 1999, on-line, Internet, November 9, 2000, available from http://www.spacedaily.com/news/gps-99f.html.

[204] "GPS Uses in Everyday Life."

Chapter 9

THE THREAT

Protection of the Marketplace

The way we make war reflects the way we make wealth.[205]

> War and Anti-War
> Alvin and Heidi Toffler
> 1993

Upon developing a source of wealth, a nation must ensure the source is protected if it desires to reap prosperity in the future. The greater the wealth, the more likely a nation will defend it—even using military power when necessary. Not defending wealth can have devastating consequences, leading to a country's demise and loss of power in the international arena. This was true for the European powers in the second millennium and it is certainly true in American history. Even before the U.S. declared its independence, it was defending one source of wealth with a navy.[206] While the role of the U.S. Navy has changed over the years, one enduring mission that remains to this day is the protection of wealth derived from international trade. The marketplace in space is large and continues to grow at a robust rate. As the U.S. continues in its attempt to command this marketplace, competition will rise and challenge this dominance. This source of wealth must also be protected like the U.S. Navy protects the maritime marketplace.

Historical Roles of U.S. Navy

By the mid-1700s, the British command of the sea extended not only from the Indian Ocean but also across the Atlantic Ocean to the shores of America. With its domination of the seas, the British were able to defend its maritime wealth. In 1775, the British threatened the American colonies' trading and this in turn threatened to wreak destruction on the seaside settlements.[207] To counter this threat to economic prosperity, the Continental Congress voted on 13 October 1775 to establish a navy with two armed sailing vessels and immediately sent them on a three-month cruise, "to intercept transports carrying munitions and stores to the British army in America."[208] In addition to this small naval force, American merchants began to arm their own ships and started a privateering campaign against British commerce. The Continental Congress laid out a clear mission for this fledgling navy; it was not to contest the British for command of the sea, "but rather to wage a traditional *guerre de course* against the British."[209] During the war for independence, the Continental Navy grew to more than 50 vessels. In the end, this small but effective force captured nearly 200 British vessels and forced the British to divert warships to protect their own convoys and trade routes. On the political front, this navy was instrumental in bringing France into the war to fight against the British.[210] For the moment, America's trade on the open seas was secure.

With the end of the war, the Continental Congress was faced with the issue of what to do with its navy. It was expensive to maintain and there did not appear to be a threat for the navy to confront. With the traditional Anglo-American fear of large standing armies and the war over, the cash-poor Congress agreed to dissolve the navy. Two years later, the last ship was sold.[211] Events in the global marketplace would soon show the short sightedness of this decision.

Following the war, America's trading routes were expanding and reached all the way to the Mediterranean. By the 1780's, American merchant ships were coming under increasing attack from the Barbary States. With protection no longer afforded by the Royal Navy and with the U.S. Navy nonexistent, ships and cargoes were captured and several U.S. seamen were ransomed or sold into slavery. Although the number of incidents was few, this violation of sovereignty caused a significant debate on how this country should protect its wealth derived from trading. Thomas Jefferson addressed this issue in the fall of 1784, "We ought to begin a naval power, if we mean to carry on our commerce."[212] While the nation did not act immediately on Jefferson's recommendation, it did highlight the apparent helplessness of this country in the global marketplace. In 1789, a new constitution was adopted and Congress was given the right "to provide and maintain" a navy. The delegates envisioned a country "powerful enough to maintain a navy capable of protecting U.S. commerce."[213] While the authorization was in place, the appropriations were lacking and so the U.S. continued without a naval force until the mid-1790s. With the outbreak of war in Europe in 1793, all of this was to change.[214]

With the advent of war, U.S. trade greatly expanded in the European theater of operations. As the number of U.S. ships increased so did the opportunity for pirating by foreign powers. In 1794, the U.S responded to the persistent attacks from the Barbary Coast corsairs by passing a naval act, which called for the construction of six frigates. With the nation's wealth increasing, the size of the navy grew to more than thirty ships by 1800. In these years, the Navy focused on convoying the merchant vessels and maintaining the sea lines of communications from raiding French and Tripolitan ships. By 1807, the role of the U.S. Navy was clearly established—protection of nation's commerce while protection of the homeland was given exclusively to the U.S. Army.[215]

With the War of 1812, Americans learned another lesson on the importance of sea power. "The commerce of the nation had been swept from the seas and its coast blockaded and subjected to raids and invasions, despite the presence of an enormous fleet of gunboats."[216] The need for a creditable, seagoing battle fleet to keep the enemy at bay became obvious to the nation. In spite of this lesson, the major post-war mission of the navy remained protection of commerce.[217] This mission remained a vital national interest as evidenced by the fact that U.S. merchant ships transported 92 percent of America's international trade in 1826.[218] During the Mexican War (1846-1848) and Civil War, the navy proved its strategic worth in gunboat diplomacy. After these wars however, its mission remained on protecting commerce and expanding U.S. markets.[219]

In the 1880s, the United States entered an era of rapid global change. As a result of the industrial revolution, European imperialism was on the rise. Euro0e was quickly expanding its political and economic influence in both Africa and Eurasia. As America looked abroad, it saw its potential overseas markets threatened. Both the Ottoman and Chinese empires, long the target of U.S. commercial interests, were ready to fall to the European powers. Closer to home, the Europeans were increasingly involved in the affairs of Central and South America. To answer these challenges, the nation looked to the navy. By the 1890s, the U.S. Navy entered a new era. The nation now recognized the navy as a full-fledged instrument of power for furthering the security and prosperity of the nation. Congress continued to see commerce as the lifeblood of a modern industrializing nation but it also saw protection of the nation as an equally important mission for the navy.[220]

With the outbreak of World War I, U.S. freedom of the seas was threaten and thus overseas commerce was at risk. The U.S. Congress responded to this threat by launching a massive ship building campaign to make a navy second to none. Although this greatly expanded navy was instrumental in achieving the allied victory, it was quickly reduced in size after the war; once again in keeping with American's fear of large standing armies. During World War II, the U.S. again embarked on an immense ship building campaign and the navy took the lead for securing the North Atlantic as well as holding the front in the Pacific.[221] After the war, there appeared to be no naval threat—the U.S. truly commanded the global seas. Even with this monumental success, naval critics were soon questioning the roles and missions of a post-war navy.

Current Roles of U.S. Navy

With the end of the World War II and the beginning of the Cold War, the forwarded-deployed navy became a first line of offense against the Soviet threat. "The shift from foreign policy to national security policy in which diplomacy and military power were closely intertwined" provided the navy with the justification needed for the carrier program.[222] These "forward-deployed, offensively capable naval forces, generally built around carrier battle groups, became symbols of U.S. commitment to its allies, most notably those in the Mediterranean and the western Pacific."[223] While the navy remained a creditable deterrent throughout the Cold War, its size and focus has changed over the years.

At the peak of the Cold War, the Secretary of the Navy sought to increase the size of the navy to 600 ships. Today, there are only 315 ships in the navy's inventory.[224] Another change for the navy is where it plans to engage national threats. In the past, the "blue water" navy sailed the open seas in defense of this country. Today, the navy is engaged in the littoral regions of the world. One mission that did not change over the years is protection of commerce. In the President's National Security Strategy, he lays out the overarching strategy for achieving America's vital national interests. A key element for increasing economic prosperity is identified—"The United States is committed to preserving internationally recognized freedom of navigation on … the world's oceans, which are critical to the future strength of our nation and maintaining global stability. Freedom of navigation … [is] essential for our economic security."[225] The Navy, recognizing the importance of this responsibility, incorporated it into its mission statement—"maintaining freedom of the seas."[226]

This responsibility, for maintaining economic security, was out played on the global arena during the President Carter years. Under the Carter Doctrine, the Soviet Union was put on notice that the U.S. would not tolerate the disruption of oil from the Persian Gulf. Then Secretary of State Muskie went further by warning the Gulf States not to interfere with the oil traffic through the Strait of Hormuz. Much of the might to back up these warnings was supplied by the expanding U.S. Naval presence in the Persian Gulf and Indian Ocean.[227]

More recently, the U.S. military as a whole was called upon to protect its economic prosperity in the Gulf War. During this war, the U.S. Navy was called upon to protect the sea lines of communication over which the allies built up their forces as well as protect the oil tankers departing from the gulf. Today, Naval forces remain in the area as a sign of our national commitment to security in the region and protection of our maritime commerce.[228] The Navy maintains the sea lines of communication for over 37,700 U.S. flagged vessels, which daily contribute to the prosperity of the nation.[229] To not protect this source of wealth would result in the loss of markets, 13.1 million jobs threatened, a decrease in the $743 billion contributed to the GDP, and finally, some of the $200 billion in federal, state, and local taxes.[230] The wealth of this nation was certainly maintained and increased due to the protection afforded by the navy.

The prosperity and security of this nation are preserved by the protection of its sources of wealth. While the navy is not the only means to protect a nation's wealth, it is certainly an effective instrument of power used today as well as in American history. To protect our national future, the nation must identify how it will defend new sources of national wealth. Just look at the e-commerce sector. In this marketplace, technology rapidly outpaced the government's ability to provide protection. As a result, it seems like every week there is one more hacker attack and thus another loss in wealth generation. At a recent supercomputer conference, leaders from civilian laboratories as well as Department of Defense were briefed on the increasing threat of viruses. By 2004, it is estimated viruses will be generated at the rate of one per hour and the annual cost to control these attacks will exceed $100 billion.[231] As the U.S. continues its quest to command space, it must seriously address the issue of space commerce protection.

The Threat to Space Wealth

In European as well as American history, if a national source of wealth was not protected, it was always challenged by a competitor. This is the law of human nature concerning wealth—everyone will attempt to get his or her hands on vulnerable treasure. The Spratly Islands provide a current case in point. The race is on by China, Taiwan, Vietnam, the Philippines, Malaysia and Brunei to be the first to exploit the petroleum resources that lie beneath the South China Sea.[232] The same is true for space. As the U.S. continues to command space, it not only enjoys the wealth and security derived from space but it also grows increasingly vulnerable. Without the ability to maintain space lines of communication, an attack becomes more inviting—especially if the competitor is not a space faring nation. Attacking a satellite or the space infrastructure provides a cost-effective, asymmetric strategy to overcome the economic and security advantage enjoyed by the United States. This threat already exists today. Many of the U.S.'s potential adversaries—Russia, China, Iran, Iraq, Cuba and North Korea—currently possess jammers to deny service.[233] In addition, U.S. intelligence officials recently testified before the Senate Intelligence Committee on the reality of the space threat. Vice Admiral Wilson, Director of the Defense Intelligence Agency, stated that by 2015, "future adversaries will be able to employ a wide variety of means to disrupt, degrade or defeat portions of the U.S. space support system."[234] In the same hearing, Mr. Tenet, Director of the CIA, characterized the space threat as growing and stated, "Operations to disrupt, degrade, or defeat U.S. space assets will be attractive options for those seeking to counter U.S. strategic military superiority."[235]

Other parts of the world are already experiencing hostile attacks. Indonesia recently jammed a transponder on a Chinese communication satellite. Both Iran and Turkey used jammers to disrupt TV broadcasts by dissidents.[236] While these examples are far from American shores, the potential exists for a jamming attack that could have catastrophic effects on this country. The Russians are currently marketing a handheld GPS jammer that can deny access out to 80 kilometers. A slightly larger version can deny GPS access out to 192 kilometers.[237]

Consider the impact to this nation if a terrorist group acquired 50 of these units and then deployed five of these units in each of America's ten largest cities. The beauty of this attack is that it can be conducted in a "fire and forget" manner. Once the units are strategically placed in financial districts as well as close to the international airports, the terrorists can leave the scene and activate the jammers remotely. This attack provides the terrorist with low exposure and high impact. Almost immediately, the financial community would be disrupted since it relies on accurate GPS timing for much of its financial transactions. It is not too far fetched to imagine a Tom Clancy *Debt of Honor* scenario, where the New York Stock Exchange is thrown into chaos as a result of this attack. In addition, many aircraft would lose their access to GPS navigation and the airports would quickly become congested. Even if the jammers were found in an hour, the damage would have already occurred and attack would have been a success. There is nothing to prevent terrorists group from conducting re-attacks since the equipment is affordable and not detectable until activated. With the easy financing available to terrorists today, this scenario is not out of the realm of possibilities.

Foreshadowings of this type of attack have already occurred in the real world. In 1998, the Air Force conducted a transmitter test that took out navigation signals for a commercial, GPS-equipped aircraft. As a result, the Federal Aviation Administration declared an interference zone of 300 kilometers.[238] These jammers not only impact civil and commercial operations but also military operations. In 2000, the Iraqis used Russian-supplied jammers to foil at least one patrol of U.S. warplanes over the no fly zones.[239] Early on, the military recognized the hostile use of GPS jammers as a serious threat and in 1993, the Joint Electronic Warfare Center began development of direction finders for GPS jammers.[240]

The ground infrastructure is just as easily attacked. One reason why the Air Force moved their satellite control centers from Sunnyvale Air Force Base, California to Schreiver Air Force Base, Colorado was due to the vulnerability of that base. With proximity of the base to California Highway 237, terrorists could easily attack the ground antennas, used for commanding and telemetry receiving, with rocket powered grenades. The attack would take less than five minutes and the terrorists could quickly depart the scene before security forces would be able to react. Had this attack occurred, the terrorists would have succeeded in severely impeding the Air Force's ability to command its satellites and thus weakened the nation's command of information. While there are no major highways outside the front gates of Schreiver, the base still remains a high value target--almost all of the Air Force's satellites are commanded from this one location. If an adversary wanted to severely degrade the nation's information superiority before a major offensive, Schreiver presents an attractive target of choice.

Of course, the satellite itself can also be attacked. For a number of years, the Russians and Chinese have worked on lasers for the purpose of blinding U.S. satellites. The Russians also have an on-orbit anti-satellite system, although it has not been operationally employed for a number of years, for disabling or destroying low earth orbiting satellites. The Chinese government recognizes the disproportionate information advantage satellites deliver in a conflict and recently announced the development of a new anti-satellite system. The Small Satellite Research Institute of the Chinese Academy of Space Technology has built a nanometer-sized "parasite satellite." When deployed, this parasite is attached to an enemy's satellite. During a conflict, commands are sent to the "parasite," which will then interfere or destroy the host satellite in less than a minute. This weapon system is envisioned for attack against comsats, early warning satellites, navsats, reconnaissance satellites; military and civilian satellites; a single satellite or constellation; a space-based laser; and even space stations. With a cost of 0.1 to 1 per cent of a typical satellite, the "parasite satellite" presents a cost effective, asymmetric weapon for weakening a nation's information superiority.[241]

All of the above attacks are to be expected in time of conflict, but another, equally threatening though silent, attack is being waged everyday—attack of marketshare. For the U.S. to improve its prosperity and security, it must apply strategic innovation in the space sector to increase its global market share. In recent years, after dominating the global space marketplace, just the opposite is happening—the U.S.'s commanding lead in this business sector is declining. An analysis of last year's performance illustrates the downward trend. For the year 2000, "exports of U.S. civil and commercial spacecraft and satellite components dropped 59 per cent," according to the Aerospace Industries Association. During this same time period, the export of military satellite hardware dropped almost 60 percent while the export of satellites dropped 4.9 percent.[242] A February 2001 report by the Satellite Industry Association confirms this loss of market share. Last year, U.S. commercial satellite builders lost $1.2 billion in contracts and 1,000 jobs[243]. This same trend is also occurring in the space launch business. In the past, the U.S. dominated this business sector but now this commerce is literally leaving the shores of this country. Increasingly, U.S. companies are looking for cheaper and available launch services and are finding other options in Russia, China, and the European Space Agency. While some of this decline is due to market forces, an equal amount of this decline is due to government regulation. For this reason, both government and industry must work together to increase the nation's prosperity and security derived from space.

A recent attack on the future marketplace illustrates the fierce international competition for additional wealth. In August 2000, the Greek government sponsored a tank competition among the British, Germans, French and U.S. The competition would determine the Greek Army's next tank and award a $1.4 billion contract to build 250 tanks. During the trials, the British and U.S. tanks, both equipped with GPS receivers, experienced multiple navigation errors. After the embarrassing performance, officials reportedly found French GPS jammers on the firing range that were remotely activated when the British and U.S. tanks were tested. Even though the Greek defense officials discounted the technical problems, the threat still remains. If an ally can cause this amount of havoc in peacetime, what effect would a hostile jamming have during combat operations?[244]

For this nation to continue its quest of commanding space, it must address this genuine threat at the national level. The Department of Defense can not solve this problem alone, rather the resources of the entire government must be harnessed. This is a national challenge and as such must be addressed by the nation as a whole—government, military, and commercial business. To remain a world superpower, the new administration and Congress must support a vision that includes the command of space.

Chapter 10

THE VISION

Why Now?

Our national courage has been clear in times of depression and war, when defending common dangers defined our common good. Now we must choose if the example of our fathers and mothers will inspire us or condemn us. We must show the courage in time of blessing by confronting problems instead of passing them on to future generations.

President George W. Bush
Inauguration speech
January 2001

During this period of relative prosperity and security, it is imperative for the nation to have a vision of the future. The following truism reminds us of the value of having a vision: "If you don't know where you are going, you will probably never reach it." An abiding national interest is to further our unprecedented blessings. However, during times of peace and prosperity, it is easy to lose sight of this goal and not pay the costs to pursue it. In addition, history shows that competitors are typically more motivated to knock off "number one" than "number one" is motivated to remain on top. To prevent a competitor from toppling this nation, the U.S. must boldly pursue a vision for commanding space. Pursuing this vision alone will not ensure continued prosperity and security but to not pursue this vision will lead to the eventual demise of U.S. dominance.

There are three important reasons why the year 2001 is a unique time in our nation's history, to pursue this vision: time of strategic pause, fiscal resources available and a new administration.

Strategic Pause

With the end of the Cold War, America entered a new era—a unipolar world in which it remains the only superpower. This country emerged not only as the world's greatest military power, but also as the world's greatest economic power. In addition, many analysts predict that the U.S. will not face another peer competitor for another 10-15 years. Today, Americans enjoy a security and prosperity unknown by many past generations. This is not to say that the military is not engaged in defense of this country. In many ways the military is even more engaged than ever before but the important difference is that it is not playing a game of strategic brinkmanship with another superpower. With the demise of the Soviet Union, the threat of nuclear destruction no longer hangs over the American society.

During this time of strategic pause, the Department of Defense must break out of the "same way of doing business" mentality and craft a plan of strategic innovation for the future. The military must address how it can best support the nation within the fiscal realities. This pause in superpower tensions offers a rare opportunity that can not be wasted. Now is the time to entertain and give serious analysis to new visions of the future. These visions must be examined by the guiding touchstone of "What is best for the country and not what is best for a service." Now is the time to give serious thought on the military's role in helping the nation command space.

One promising achievement in defining the military's role for commanding space occurred in January 2001. For one week, 250 participants played at the Air Force's Space Warfare Center in "the military's first major war game to focus on space as the primary theater of operations, rather than just a supporting arena for combat on the earth."[245] While this milestone is laudable, it must be balanced by the fact that space for the U.S. military has been around since 1958. In addition, there are no Joint Chiefs of Staff publications, which define how the services will fight in combat, dedicated to space combat or even space operations. These examples are not an indictment against the military but rather illustrate the amount of work that lies ahead. During this time of strategic pause is the time to define how the military will aid in nation's quest to command space.

Government Surplus

Any national quest involves the expenditure of national treasure—time, people, and capital. Without these components, the quest can not begin. The quest to opening any marketplace is a particularly costly venture, which in the beginning appears daunting. For all the seed money invested to launch new businesses, only ten percent of the new ventures succeed.[246] Without a profitable return on investment, there is little incentive for a nation to pay such a high cost. The quest to command space is no different; it will be an expensive venture. Fortunately, this country is currently enjoying a federal budget surplus and it is projected that this luxury will continue for a number of years.

According to the FY 2001 Federal Budget, the current surplus is estimated at over $2.9 trillion over the 2001-2010 time period. The Clinton administration chose to strengthen the security of this nation by allocating the vast majority of this money toward reducing the national debt and fortifying the solvency of the Social Security. However, over this same time period, $16 billion remains unallocated.[247] The good news on the surplus continues. In December 2000, the Congressional Budget Office revised the 10-year surplus up to $6 trillion.[248] With this number, President Bush can carry out his proposed $1.6 trillion tax cut, continue the 10-year plan laid out in the 2001 budget and still have money left over—roughly $1.5 trillion. Even allowing for an overestimation of $1 trillion, $500 billion is unallocated over the next ten years. The challenge for the Bush administration is how to wisely spend this money in pursuit of our national interests.

New Administration

Whenever there is a "changing of the guard" at the national level, there is an opportunity for new visions and direction. Independent of political parties, every administration comes in with new ideas on how the nation can best be served. In the run up to the election, then-Governor Bush laid out his plans for the military in a speech given at the Citadel. His three goals were to "renew the bond of trust between the American president and the American military; ... defend the American people against missiles and terror; and ... begin creating the military of the next century."[249] The last two objectives will certainly impact the advancement of space. Later on his speech, he further elaborated on his intentions for space. On his second objective, he stated his commitment to deploy at the soonest possible date a theater and national ballistic missile system, whether the Russians agree or not. While elaborating on the third goal, he stated, "in space, we must be able to protect our network of satellites, essential to the flow of our commerce and the defense of our country."[250] In the few short months that he has been in office, President Bush has already begun to deliver on this election promises.

National Missile Defense clearly appears to have moved from the "slow burner" of the previous administration to the "fast track." Even though international controversy has arisen, the president does not appear dissuaded in his cause. On the protection of satellites, his resolve is not as clearly seen. However, there are indications that he is also going ahead "full steam" on this initiative also. In Washington, it was reported that the nation's policy for space is shifting from a focus on exploration and commercial development to one dominated by war fighters. The military is not missing this cue and General Eberhart, who is commander over all of the military's space forces, recently gave a briefing on the armed forces role in protecting satellites on orbit.[251] With the president's appointment of Donald Rumsfeld, who chaired the recent Space Commission, as the Secretary of Defense, space and its advancement is certainly to remain on the president's agenda. Now is the time to propose a bold vision that will support the president's goals for the military. If the military fails to step up to this challenge, it has failed in its service to the Commander in Chief and ultimately, to the nation.

Notes

[205] Alvin and Heidi Toffler, *War and Anti-War, Survival at the Dawn of the 21st Century*, (Boston: Little, Brown and Company, 1993), 3.

[206] Michael A. Palmer, "The Navy," March 31, 1997, 2; on-line, Internet, December 13, 2000, available from http://www.history.navy.mil/history/history1.htm.

[207] "The Birth of the Navy of the United States," October 4, 2000, 2; on-line, Internet, January 17, 2001, available from http://www.history.navy.mil/faqs/faqs31-1.htm.

[208] Ibid.

[209] Michael A. Palmer, "The Navy: The Continental Period, 1775-1890," December 19, 1996, 7; on-line, Internet, December 13, 2000, available from http://www.history.navy.mil/history/history2.htm.

[210] "The Birth of the Navy of the United States."

[211] Michael A. Palmer, "The Navy: The Continental Period, 1775-1890."

[212] Ibid.

[213] Ibid.

[214] Ibid.

Notes

[215] Ibid.

[216] Ibid.

[217] Ibid.

[218] "Seapower/MARITIME," 19; on-line, Internet, January 23, 2001, available from http://www.navyleague.org/seapower/seapower_maritime.htm.

[219] Michael A. Palmer, "The Navy: The Continental Period, 1775-1890."

[220] Michael A. Palmer, "The Navy: The Oceanic Period, 1890-1945," December 19, 1996, 4; on-line, Internet, December 13, 2000, available from http://www.history.navy.mil/history/history3.htm.

[221] Ibid.

[222] Ibid.

[223] Ibid.

[224] "Status of the United States Navy," January 22, 2001, 2; on-line, Internet, January 24, 2001, available from http://www.chinfo.navy.mil/navpalib/news/.www/status.html.

[225] White House, *A National Security Strategy For A New Century*, December 1999, 12.

[226] The full mission statement of the Navy: "The mission of the Navy is to maintain, train, and equip combat-ready Naval forces capable of winning wars, deterring aggression and maintaining freedom of the seas." "Navy Organization," 1; on-line, Internet, January 17, 2001, available from http://www.chinfo.navy.mil/navpalib/organization/org-top.html.

[227] Michael A. Palmer, "The Navy: The Transoceanic Period, 1945-1992" December 19, 1996, 4; on-line, Internet, December 13, 2000, available from http://www.history.navy.mil/history/history4.htm.

[228] Ibid.

[229] "New Marad Report Shows Size, Scope of U.S.-Flag Fleet," January 13, 2000, 2; on-line, Internet, December 13, 2000, available from http://www.dot.gov/affairs/marad0100.htm.

[230] Maritime commerce, creates 13.1 million jobs, contributes $743 billion to the gross domestic product, and provides almost $200 billion in federal, state, and local taxes. U.S. ports handle more than two billion tons of foreign and domestic trade. "Seapower/MARITIME," *The 2000 Almanac of Seapower*, January 2000, 19; online, Internet, January 23, 2001, available from http://www.navyleague.org/seapower/seapower_maritime.html.

[231] Eugene Spafford, director of Purdue's Center for Education and Research in Information Assurance and Security delivered the referenced brief at the supercomputing SC2000 conference. Patricia Daukantas, "Feds show off bulk-up plans for supercomputing muscle," *Government Computer News*, January 22, 2001, 29.

[232] "China's First Aircraft Carrier Ready for Service in 2005: Report," January 12, 2000, 1; on-line, Internet, February 5, 2001, available from http://taiwansecurity.org/AFP/AFP-01122000-Aircraft-Carrier.htm.

[233] *Commission to Assess United States National Security Space Management and Organization*, January 11, 2001, 19-20.

Notes

[234] Bill Gertz, "Space seen as battlefield of future," February 8, 2001, 3; on-line, Internet, February 9, 2001, available from http://www.washtimes.com/national/default-20012823833.htm.

[235] Ibid.

[236] *Commission to Assess United States National Security Space Management and Organization*, January 11, 2001, 19-20.

[237] Ibid. There are two basic types of jammers. One is a noise jammer that disrupts the GPS downlink. This is the type the Russians are selling. Another type of jamming is spoofing. A GPS spoofer emits erroneous data and confuses the navigation receiver. According to Lincoln Labs, a one-watt spoofer placed at Boston's Logan Airport would corrupt the GPS signal for 300 miles. Imagine the impact to military operations if spoofers were placed in a combat zone where GPS-guided munitions were being dropped. The bombs would go awry and CNN as well as the adversary would have a field day. Remember all the fall out from the Chinese Embassy being attacked during the Operation Allied Force? "A Presentation to the Air Navigation Commission of The International Civil Aviation Organization," February 23, 2000, 4; on-line, Internet, January 25, 2001, available from http://www.aopa.de/letter/loran%20and%20gps.html.

[238] Bob Brewin, "Rogue transmitter knocks out GPS signals," April 13, 1998, 4; on-line, Internet, January 25, 2001, available from http://208.201.97.5/pubs/fcw/1998/0413/fcw-frontgps-4-13-1998.html.

[239] Simon Saradzhyan, "Iraq Jamming Missiles With Russian Device," July 18, 2000, 2; on-line, Internet, January 25, 2001, available from http://www.sptimes.ru/archive/times/586/news/n_iraq.htm.

[240] Henry Spencer, "Space News from Aug 30, 1993 AW&ST," 4; on-line, Internet, January 25, 2001, available from http://www.islandone.org/SpencerAvLeakReports/AvWeek-930830.html.

[241] Ground tests with this system have proven this concept and are very effective in their intended operations. The Chinese have long-term as well as short-term objectives for this weapon system. The long-term objectives include "establish a strategic balance among the larger nations, and to break up the monopoly on utilization of space that large space systems of the superpowers are holding; thus weakening their capabilities in information warfare." For the short term, "China would strengthen its capability in controlling the usage of space globally, and change drastically the Chinese-American military balance so that U.S. would not intervene easily in the event of a conflict in the Taiwan Strait and at the Chinese perimeter." Cheng Ho, "China Eyes Anti-Satellite System," *SpaceDaily*, January 8, 2000, 3; on-line, Internet, January 8, 2001, available from http//www.spacer.com/news/china-01c.html.

[242] For the year 2000, space exports were down in the following categories: components, from $410 to $170 million; military hardware, from $369 to $150 million; and satellites, from $151 to $144 billion. Lon Rains and Stew Mannuson, "U.S. Satellite Exports Drop 59 Percent," December 14, 2000, 2; on-line, Internet, available from http://www.space.com/businesstechnology/business/aia_report_001214.html.

[243] Vernon Loeb, "Back Channels: Satellite Woes," *Washington Post*, February 6, 2001, 15.

Notes

[244] The referenced article is based on 6 August 2000 reports in *The Sunday Times of London*, Agence France-Presse and the 25 September 2000 *Elevtheros Tipos*, Athens. Lt. Col. Lester W. Grau, U.S. Army, Retired, "GPS Signals Jammed During Tank Trials," *Military Review*, March-April 2001, 12.

[245] This exercise was called Schreiver 2001. Thomas E. Ricks, "Space Is Playing Field For Newest War Game," *Washington Post*, January 29, 2001, 1.

[246] Dr. Grant Hammond, Air War College Faculty, notes to author, 22 February 2001.

[247] Office of Management and Budget, *Budget of the United States, Fiscal Year 2001*, (Washington DC: U.S. Government Printing Office, 2000), 391.

[248] Jonathan Weisman, "Surplus soars despite slump," *USA Today*, 22-25 December 2000, 1.

[249] Ron Fournier, "Bush Seeks $20B for New Weapons," September 23, 1999, 2; on-line, Internet, February 21, 2001, available from http://www.prop1.org/nucnews/9909nn/990923nn.htm.

[250] Governor George W. Bush, "A Period of Consequences" speech, September 23, 1999, 6; on-line, Internet, February 21, 2001, available from http://www.gop.com/GWbushpages/gw_periodofconse.asp.

[251] Larry Wheeler, "Military Space Role Already Growing Under Bush," 3; on-line, Internet, February 13, 2001, available from http://www.space.com/missionlaunches/missions/fl_bush_010209.html.

Chapter 11

The Evolution of the Vision of Space

Like the great nations of the past that controlled the land and the seas, America's future security and prosperity depend on our constant supremacy in space. While we are ahead of any potential rival in exploiting space, we are not unchallenged. To ensure superiority, we must combine expansive thinking with a sustained commitment of resources and vest them in a dedicated, independent proponent for space.[252]

Senator Bob Smith
January 2001

Space isn't just a matter of national prestige, although that is important too, space means the latest technology that is the foundation of the competitiveness of the economy and the security of our nation. Space, without exaggeration, is the foundation for stability in the world.[253]

Vladimir Putin
Russian Federation President
January 30, 2001

The year 2001, is frequently associated with the movie 2001 A Space Odyssey. This title implies an extended, adventurous journey in space.[254] The question that arises, is "A quest to where, to what end, for what purpose?" All the space-faring countries of the world are concentrating on these questions and are developing national visions in response. For 2001, China has set an aggressive quest of putting a manned spacecraft into orbit, completing an indigenous space navigation constellation, and launching a total of 30 satellites in the next five years.[255] In the face of the U.S.'s proposed development of National Missile Defense, Russia is pursing an aggressive space vision and has threatened to begin another space/arms race in response. Meanwhile, the European Union appears to be going ahead with plans to develop and field Galileo, a European challenge to the U.S.'s Global Positioning System. In Jan 2001, the Italian Parliament approved $291 million funding toward the $1 billion project.[256] Even the non-spacefaring country of Vietnam has announced plans to build satellites within the next decade.[257] The United States is not being left in behind in this quest for space. In 2001, this country is formulating a national space vision on how the nation's prosperity and security goals will be met in the future.

With the beginning of the new millennium, many members in Congress began to question where the nation was headed in the space arena. There were growing concerns that the nation lacked a clear vision for the future. This skepticism was not confined to the Department of Defense but also included the national, civil and commercial space sectors. In 2000, three separate commissions were created to address this lack of vision.

The first congressional mandated study was the Independent Commission on the National Imagery and Management Agency (NIMA). NIMA is a Department of Defense (DoD) combat support agency that provides imagery to the military, national policy makers and civil users.[258] Satellites, to include national, civil, and commercial, collect much of the imagery exploited by NIMA, for intelligence and geospatial information. While the Commission concluded, "NIMA is an essential component of U.S. national security and a key to information dominance" it did make a number of recommendations on how to better manage the imagery information process, namely tasking, processing, exploitation, and dissemination.[259] A new vision was given and only time will tell if the nation will realize the promise of NIMA's information dominance.

The second congressional study was the National Commission for the Review of the National Reconnaissance Office (NRO). The NRO, also a DoD agency, develops, acquires, and operates the nation's space reconnaissance satellites which include imagery intelligence, signals intelligence, and measurement and signature intelligence.[260] The NRO's mission "is to enable U.S. global information superiority, during peace through war."[261] The Commission concluded that the winning of the Cold War has lead to a false sense of security and as such, there is a lack of clear vision for the future of this organization. The overall conclusion recommended the President, Secretary of Defense and the Director of the Central Intelligence Agency must give their personal attention to the NRO if their mission of "global information superiority" is to be realized in the future.[262]

The final space study conducted in 2000, was the Commission to Assess United States National Security Space Management and Organization. While this study primarily focused on DoD and Intelligence Community space activities, the study also considered the role of civil and commercial space activities.[263] Once again, a bold vision was laid out that breaks the paradigm of continuing space business as usual. It is hoped that the Commission's chairman, Donald H. Rumsfeld, now Secretary of Defense, will be successful in implementing this vision of advancing the nation's national security through the advancement of space.

All three of these commissions lay out a vision that if followed will advance the prosperity and security of this nation. It is worth mentioning that another commission, The United States Commission on National Security/21st Century, was in progress during this same timeframe although it's focus was not on the advancement of space. Even so, this commission still made recommendations on how space could be enhanced to support the national security challenges of the 21st century.

It is apparent from the number of commissions reviewing space that it is a vast and complex subject. One report alone will not provide the "all encompassing" vision for where and how space can be advanced. The intent of this chapter is not to repeat or review the four aforementioned reports but rather identify new areas for advancing space. The vision presented here does not represent a new direction but rather dovetails with the already completed reports. The timeframe of this vision is the near to mid-term and implementation of many of the recommendations can be implemented in concert with the other commissions' advice.

Chapter 12

Presidential Lead

Now is the time to take longer strides—time for a great new American enterprise—time for this nation to take a clearly leading role in space achievement, which in many ways, may hold the key to our future on earth. ... I therefore ask the Congress, above and beyond the increases I have earmarked for space activity, to provide funds which are needed to meet the following goals: First, I believe that this nation should commit itself to achieving the goal, before this decade is out, of landing a man on the moon and returning him safely to earth. No single space project in this period will be more impressive to mankind ... And none will be so difficult or expensive to accomplish.[264]

President John F. Kennedy
Speech to joint session of Congress
to address "urgent national needs"
May 25, 1961

A common strength of all great civilizations of the past is that they possessed bold leaders with strategic vision. These leaders were able to assess the international arena and "see" the future—see what was best for the prosperity and security of the people. This is not to say that every leader from great civilizations possessed this ability, but rather that there were a few key leaders who either raised the civilization to prominence or maintained it. Whether the national leaders were kings, generals, or statesmen they were all able to envision the future.

American history is no different. George Washington achieved greatness in commanding the Continental Army, where against all odds, he defeated the vastly superior British Army. He then went on to become the first president, a leader who stood for and envisioned the fulfillment of the nation's founding principles. Thomas Jefferson, the third president, was also another great leader with vision. His talent was best demonstrated first in his composition of the Declaration of Independence and then in his foresight to more than double the size of the nation in the Louisiana Purchase. Abraham Lincoln, the 16th president, was another man of bold vision. He accurately foresaw this nation's well being could only be furthered if all men in this country were free and so he delivered this vision, against immense protest, fighting a civil war to preserve the Union and in issuing the Emancipation Proclamation. While these early leaders were critical to the formation of this great nation, there are others who have since helped to preserve it.

In recent history, the Cold War stands as one of the greatest threats to the preservation of this country—at times it appeared America's very existence was in question. What this nation needed was a leader with vision to preserve the security of this nation and at the same time advance the prosperity of the people. Three presidents, Eisenhower, Kennedy, and Reagan were instrumental in winning the Cold War. Their success was due in part to pulling technology, specifically space technology, to further the security of this nation.

Eisenhower: Eyes in the Sky

It was on Eisenhower watch, in 1957, that Sputnik, the world's first artificial satellite, was successfully orbited by the Soviets. Public reaction to this event bordered on hysteria. To many, this Soviet triumph posed a challenge to the U.S.'s technological supremacy and political creditability around the world. Others looked at this event as a prophetic warning of the nation's security directly being challenged. "In addition to demonstrating that the U.S. homeland was now vulnerable to Soviet intercontinental ballistic missiles (ICBMs), it also raised the less tangible fear that the United States would somehow become "blackmailed" or "dominated" from space."[265] The *New York Times* declared the U.S. was in a "race for survival" while in the House of Representatives, they talked of the prospect of "national extinction."[266] At the same time, the U-2, which was one of the few means of gathering intelligence on the Soviet Union, was becoming increasingly vulnerable to attack while over flying the Soviet landmass.

Public and congressional pressure continued to mount, demanding a national response to Sputnik. The media and the armed services responded by waged a highly vocal campaign for development of space weapons, namely orbital bombardment, ballistic missile defense, and anti-satellites. All of these programs echoed a common theme, a call for the U.S. to "gain 'space superiority' or take the 'high ground' in space or 'deny' its use to an adversary."[267] In just six weeks following the launch of Sputnik, the Army presented its plans for an anti-satellite weapon.[268] It was amid this chaos that President Eisenhower was looked to for vision and action.

As history would later show, President Eisenhower correctly viewed Soviet satellite reconnaissance as well as orbital bombardment as a limited threat to the U.S. However, "the most influential determinant of Eisenhower's space policy [was] the need to preserve the principle and later practice of satellite reconnaissance."[269] He was committed to the belief that reconnaissance satellites were of more value to the U.S. than to the Soviets. This conviction later proved to be invaluable in the area of arms control verification.[270] Due to concern over the poor management and slow progress of satellite reconnaissance, Eisenhower authorized the creation of the National Reconnaissance Office (NRO) in August 1960. This office initially combined the satellite reconnaissance efforts of the

CIA and Air Force in the Corona/Discoverer program. Eventually, this office would also incorporate the reconnaissance activities of the Navy and the National Security Agency.[271]   The NRO was directly responsible for developing the nation's "eyes and ears in space" which would constantly monitor the Soviet Union throughout the entire Cold War. Eisenhower accurately envisioned that technology could be pulled not only to develop Armageddon-type weapons but also the space systems to monitor these weapons. These systems allowed the national leadership to get inside the adversary's Observe-Orient-Decide-Act loop because of the information collected. While the information was neither 100 per cent accurate nor complete, it did afford information dominance. Information from a closed society was made available because the national leadership pulled space technology and as a result, the security of this nation was enhanced. Because of Eisenhower's firm direction, space technology continued to be pulled in the Kennedy administration.

Kennedy: Race to the Moon

At the onset of the Kennedy administration, space technology, international politics and national security were rapidly converging like never before. The two superpowers were locked in an explicit competition that was being played out on the world arena.[272] One of the first battles waged was the Soviet's opposition to satellite reconnaissance. In the summer of 1961, Kennedy and the State Department began a campaign to legitimize satellite overflight in the UN General Assembly. Kennedy's aim was to protect the nation's stake in space just as the European navies of old protected their respective claims. In December 1961, the UN approved the formal registration of space objects in space. While this milestone acknowledged overflight by satellites, it did not resolve the issue of satellite reconnaissance.[273]

In June 1962, the Soviets introduced a proposal to the UN to ban U.S. satellite reconnaissance. Recognizing the importance of satellite reconnaissance and the inherent information afforded, Kennedy began to personally lobby our closest allies to support reconnaissance from space. This strategy proved to be very successful and our allies were not taken in by the Soviet's rhetoric when they protested. In September 1963, the Soviets stopped their formal opposition since the Kosmos reconnaissance satellite was up and operational.[274] Kennedy successfully prevented the Soviets from taking the technological lead by continuing the nation's reconnaissance program, in the midst of international opposition, and by legitimizing space reconnaissance through the UN. America's satellite reconnaissance program was safe but the nation's lead in space was less secure.

Even with one battle won, the Soviet's "widely heralded triumphs … were creating 'a dangerous impression of unchallenged world leadership generally and scientific pre-eminence particularly.'"[275] With the apparent space gap growing and the latest embarrassment of Yuri Gagarin's flight in space, President Kennedy personally got involved in the nation's vision for space exploitation. Almost immediately after Gagarin's flight, Kennedy tasked his special counsel and confident, Theodore Sorensen; "Find out when, at what point, we can overtake the Russians. How long is this going to continue?"[276] On 14 April 1961, two days after Gagarin's space flight, Kennedy's key space advisors briefed him on options for going to the Moon. From the briefing several realities became apparent: 1) the Soviets held the early lead in the race to the Moon, 2) to go to the Moon would be a phenomenal engineering challenge, it would be the equivalent of another Manhattan Project, 3) the budget would be astronomical, estimates were $40 billion and 4) there was only a 50-50 chance of landing men of the Moon first and this would require an all-out effort. That evening, in conference with his special counsel, the President made the decision to go to the Moon.[277]

Science was no longer driving technology development; international politics and the quest for global power were driving it. President Kennedy's vision pulled space technology to reestablish America as the world's greatest nation. Landing a man on the Moon was the only peaceful way to reinstill confidence in the American public. Initially, he wavered in his conviction to go to the Moon. He even asked one advisor if there were any other scientific challenges that were just as dramatic and convincing. Even so, Kennedy in his deliberations reasoned that a secondary consequence of this decision was the creation of jobs and feeding of a young aerospace industry.[278] As the day approached for his 25 May "Landing a man on the Moon" speech, he grew resolute in his conviction. In the days leading up to the famous speech, the National Security Advisor recommended against this goal and yet the President held firm.[279]

Kennedy's vision began to come to pass on the morning of 16 July 1969, when Apollo 11 left the Earth. Four days later, the same amount of time required by Jules Verne's spacecraft, Astronaut Armstrong announced, "'Houston, Tranquility Base here. The Eagle has landed.'"[280] In this one triumph, America firmly reestablished its global dominance. Although thousands supported this vision and made it happen, only one man made the strategic decision to go to the Moon, President Kennedy. The Cold War would continue but for the moment, America basked in its newfound security and prosperity.

Reagan: Star Wars

Many military members remember the Reagan presidency as the "golden years." Here was an era where no military project was too large or ambitious in countering the "Evil Empire."[281] One need only recall the superpowers' arms race of the 1980s and early 90s: main battle tank, T-72 versus M1, then T-80 versus M1A1; air superiority, MiG-25 versus F-15; new bomber, Backfire versus B-1 and even in space, Buran versus the Space Shuttle and competing anti-satellite systems (ASAT).[282] As a result of this race, the military-industrial complex experienced significant growth and prosperity. Here was a president who firmly believed that technology was the key to ensuring national security.[283] And yet, the Soviets were able to match America "tit for tat" in terms of weapon systems and global influence. The dilemma that lay before the president was how to restore national security and prosperity. President Reagan would ultimately turn to space technology for answers.

In the presidential race leading up to the 1980 election, then Governor Reagan toured the North American Aerospace Defense Command Headquarters located deep within Cheyenne Mountain. He was stunned to learn that the country had no means to protect itself from a ballistic missile attack, not even one missile.[284] This significant emotional event stayed with him throughout his presidency and ultimately shaped his space policy. From the beginning of his presidency, Reagan recognized the importance of space for the nation and as a result remained directly involved in its development. Eight months after taking office, Reagan began to change the course of space development. In August 1981, the Reagan administration rejected a Soviet offer to discuss a draft UN proposal on space weapons. This was followed by Secretary of Defense Weinberger's announcement on 5

October that the U.S. would continue to pursue an operational ASAT system.[285]   In addition, Reagan's space policy also called for projection of force in and from space.[286] President Reagan's ultimate space vision would not materialize until March 23, 1983.

In his now famous "Star Wars" speech, he announced plans to proceed with research on ballistic missile defense. The main thrust of the speech called for increased military funding and only toward end did he announce his intention to "embark on a program to counter the awesome Soviet missile threat with measures that are defensive."[287] He called upon the scientific and engineering community to aid in this quest, "those who gave us nuclear weapons to turn their great talent now to the cause of mankind and world peace: to give us the means of rendering these nuclear weapons impotent and obsolete."[288] The technical community fervently responded to this presidential call to arms. Soon there were designs for all types of grandiose space weapons: rail guns, brilliant pebbles, X-ray fired lasers, directed energy weapons, on-orbit surveillance systems, and constellations of orbiting mirrors to direct terrestrial laser firings. Even though billions of dollars were expended in this quest and no hardware was deployed into space, it arguably won the Cold War.

Reagan's Strategic Defense Initiative (SDI) was the straw that broke the Soviet's back. While this event alone did not bring about the collapse of the Soviet Union, it certainly aided in as well as sped up the downfall of this rival superpower. While the scientists provided the technical details and Congress the budget, President Reagan alone gets the credit for pursuing this Cold War-winning strategy. The Star Wars speech caught everyone in ballistic missile research by surprise and even Secretaries Weinberger and Schultz were only told in the final stages of its preparation. The Presidential Science Advisor noted afterwards: "This was not a speech that came up; it was a top down speech … a speech that came from the President's heart."[289] While the Cold War is over, America's quest for greater prosperity and security continues on.

Spacelift: The "Holy Grail" of Space

The 21st century begins with a new president confronting the same space challenges of the past—what is the role of space in providing for the national well being? President Bush is cognizant of this issue and is already addressing it. Even though it may not capture the imagination of the American public, President Bush's initiative to build a National Missile Defense (NMD) is in some ways similar to President Kennedy's challenge to go to the Moon. It is also a rebirth of President's Reagan's vision for providing ballistic missile defense for the nation. President Bush's commitment is one that impacts the whole nation, even if no missiles are launched. It will be extremely expensive, latest estimates are $60 billion,[290] and space technology will certainly be "pulled" forward to meet new national security requirements. In addition, this program will reinvigorate the faltering aerospace industry by providing thousands of high-tech, high-paying jobs. On the international scene, both Russia and China express concerns of another arms race as well as the European Union to a lesser degree.[291] In the end, this grand, national challenge will ensure new security as well as new prosperity. President Bush, along with Secretary of Defense Rumsfeld, is taking the appropriate lead for this monumental project. The leader of the nation must show his commitment to a national program if it is to receive the necessary funding and thus have a successful start.

While President Bush is certainly showing presidential leadership in this space venture, there is another space endeavor that requires his attention. This issue is the greatest technical barrier to commanding space and its resolution will do more to advance the nation's quest than any other issue. The technical challenge is the lack of ready, reliable, and affordable spacelift. One look at the U.S.'s rocket booster development reveals just how long this enabling technology has been neglected. The United States developed only one new booster rocket in the last twenty years, while Russia developed and tested more than 140.[292]

With a rate of $10,000 per pound to low earth orbit,[293] a satellite must literally be worth more than its weight in gold. For some space systems, over half the cost is wrapped up in getting the satellite on orbit.[294] With these astronomical rates, the U.S. conducts far too few space launches to tackle the related challenges of readiness and reliability. By conducting more launches, both issues can be resolved but this is only possible if launch costs are drastically reduced. To ensure national security and prosperity for the 21st century, the cost of spacelift must decrease. In short, the high access cost prevents true command of space.

The importance of reducing launch costs for national security was graphically illustrated in the Schreiver 2001 wargame. In this wargame, the "Blue" or friendly (U.S. and allies) team received intelligence that the "Red" or adversary team was preparing to fire ground-based lasers at Blue's on-orbit space assets. At this point, the game participants were faced with a strategic decision, absorb Red's strikes or launch a preemptive strike? Based on lessons learned from a previous year's wargame, the participants launched an "early deterrence strike" against Red. Rather than stopping the crisis, the deterrence strike had just the opposite effect—Red viewed the action as provative and began the war. One game participant noted that the Blue team had no other choice since it had no other way to protect its space assets.[295] The Chairman of the Joint Chiefs of Staff, as the president's primary military advisor, must convey the limitations of protecting U.S. satellites to the president. One can only hope that this outcome will have the same searing effect on President Bush that the lack of a national ballistic missile defense had on President Reagan.

If the cost for spacelift is reduced from half to 15-20 percent of a space system, a different outcome for the wargame is possible.[296] In a real life scenario, the president must be presented with more options than immediately going to war over a satellite attack. The real world response to this wargame also echoes this opinion. Chinese officials blasted this wargame in which they said, the U.S. was the blue team coming to the aid of Taiwan against China, the red team. A Chinese military expert in Beijing warned that China should prepare for military battles with the U.S. in space.[297] The exercise's early deterrence strikes are seen in the real world as provocative and not as deterrence. With greatly reduced launch costs, the president would also have the option of rapid reconstitution. With this capability, the president, upon indications of a possible strike on U.S. space assets, could order a space plane to loiter over the intended target. Upon confirmation of an adversary's space strike, the president could immediately authorize a retaliatory strike. At the same time, launch of a replacement satellite would be authorized. Since there is a delay between launch and a fully operational satellite, the president could tap into commercial and/or allied space assets to take up the temporary slack.

Greatly reducing the cost of spacelift allows for routine space operations in time of crisis. With this capability, the military could also launch timely offensive-weapon-capable satellites to hold the adversary's satellites hostage.[298] With this option, the President need not resort to a "fire first" policy but rather engage in diplomatic diplomacy first—"you are holding our satellites hostage and we are holding your satellites hostage." While this strategy only works if the hostile nation is dependent on space assets for information, it does provide true alternative options for the president. Not only is the security of the nation greatly enhanced with reduced launch costs but it is also the key to prosperity from space.

Over the next five years, the worldwide demand for satellites will soar. It is estimated that 1,000 to 1,500 satellites, worth $500 billion, will be launched internationally during this period.[299] During this same timeframe, roughly $100 billion will be invested/returned from space annually for the U.S. In addition, $1.5 trillion in space spin-offs will be added to the U.S. economy.[300] For the U.S. to remain competitive in this marketplace and thus capture a larger share of the future space wealth, the country must embark on a quest to reduce the cost of launch. Recent history shows other countries are aggressively pursuing this lucrative market. In the mid-80s the U.S.'s launch market share was 100 percent.[301] However, by 2000 the Federal Aviation Administration reported the U.S. market share for commercial launches worldwide had dropped to 28.5 percent.[302] Vast amounts of wealth await the country that is most competitive in space. In addition, huge potential markets await the first country that develops affordable launch. Some of the new markets that are seriously being considered are power generation in space, space tourism, nuclear waste disposal, and biomedical research.[303]   Reduced launch costs are the key to remaining in the current space marketplace and for opening new markets. The questions that remain are "What is the goal?" and "How can it be achieved?"

In 1994, President Clinton signed the National Space Transportation Policy, which assigned NASA the lead for the development of low-cost, reusable launch vehicles (RLV). The RLV program's aim is to revitalize the nation's space transportation capabilities and at the same time recapture the worldwide commercial space markets. In 2000, NASA set the following formal goals: 1) by 2010, reduce the cost to low earth orbit from $10,000 per pound to $1,000, 2) by 2025, further reduce the cost to $100 and 3) by 2040, reduce the cost to tens of dollars per pound. In addition to these cost goals, the Agency also committed to concurrently improving reliability and safety several orders of magnitude.[304] This is an admirable roadmap that should be applied to expendable launch vehicles (ELV). However, recent events cast doubt on whether NASA is on track.

To reach the first goal, NASA embarked on a series of three experimental vehicles, X-33, X-34, and X-37. In March 2001, NASA cancelled development of the first two vehicles due to technical risk.[305] While it is admirable that NASA is able to make the tough decisions, it is questionable whether they are providing the necessary management. Both programs had run at least five years before they were cancelled. Now, with nine years left to reach the $1,000 per pound goal, only the X-37 remains in the race.[306] While the X-37 may be the ultimate answer, competition between designs and contractors is lost. In addition, NASA is now putting all of its eggs in one basket. NASA's chief scientist wisely testified before Congress recently that "any attempt to address a market such as launch service with a point solution is doomed to failure."[307] If NASA waits five years before making another critical program decision, there will be little time left to start with a new contractor and design to reach the first goal. One NASA strategy that has potential to reinvigorate space launch is the Space Launch Initiative (SLI). However, recent events also cast doubt on the program management.

NASA launched SLI in 2000 as a $4.5 billion, five-year program to aid human spaceflight missions, expand the commercial market in space, and support U.S. military operations in space. Since then, NASA is accused of losing sight of the primary objective, achieving affordable access to space. In addition, NASA's focus on manned spaceflight is driving commercial development away from the country's greatest need— reducing the launch cost of unmanned spacecraft. Congressman Rohrabacher stated in April 2001 that at this point, "there is no market-driven business case for a human-rated launch system."[308] As a result of this controversy, the chairman of a House space subcommittee is rightly calling for hearings, to ensure that NASA is properly spending the funds in accordance with the original objectives. The SLI program is also under attack since NASA's recently revealed that the International Space Station is $4 billion over budget. To cover this overrun, President Bush has proposed a space station without a habitation module or an escape craft. Others are suggesting the cancellation of the SLI for five years to cover these overruns.[309] This last proposal would amount to eating the seed corn for future space transportation advancement and thus slowing the U.S.'s quest to expand the commercial space market. Given this current state of affairs, President Bush's leadership is called for to get the development of space transportation back on track.

There are several actions that the president can take immediately. The first is the replacement of NASA's administrator Dan Goldin. He is a lame duck administrator left over from the Clinton administration. As such, he has been ineffective in running the Agency and this has given the Office of Management and Budget more leverage in reengineering NASA's budget.[310] The president needs to select a Wernher von Braun type of an individual to be the next administrator. This individual must possess vision, technical acumen as well as effective leadership abilities. The president should charge the new administrator with balancing the requirements for manned as well as unmanned spaceflight. Next, the administrator should be charged with looking for ways to advance the space transportation development timeline. In addition to utilizing all of NASA's resources, he should coordinate his efforts for lower launch costs with the Department of Defense's space offices. As this nation enters the 21st century, the nation can ill-afford an administrator who is not qualified for the job. The second action the president can take is to call for an annual review of the space transportation development. Congress would hold these reviews to assess the progress made to date and the amount of funds expended. A third action is to submit legislation to provide for broad-based financial and tax incentives for development of commercial space vehicles.[311] This support could take the form of tax credits, spaceport-bonding authority, tax-free bonds or even zero-g, zero tax legislation. The goal is to create an industry that is not dependent on government subsidies, but rather an industry that is subject to the free competitive marketplace.[312] A fourth action that requires urgent presidential attention is the advancement of ELVs. Currently the Air Force is only engaged in one major, new rocket design—Evolved Expendable Launch Vehicle (EELV). While this is a start in the right direction, the

Department of Defense, as the designated lead, must encourage further commercial development. Perhaps an SLI-like program is one answer. In addition, the DOD needs to set hard goals on launch cost reduction similar to NASA's. The DOD should also be held accountable to Congress and report their progress twice a year. A fifth and final action is applicable to both NASA and the DOD. Both NASA and DOD research and development (R&D) budgets have declined in recent years. With this decline, the future of U.S. space transportation looks very dim. This trend can be turned around with increased budgetary support for generic and focused R&D program for space transportation, especially rocket propulsion.[313]

Without presidential attention, the high cost to space will not be solved at a rate that will allow the U.S. to command space. Other nations are seeking to increase their share of wealth from space and so bold leadership is called for to maintain and expand the space marketplace. As the amount of wealth invested in space increases, the mission of protecting these assets becomes increasingly vital. By addressing the challenge of space launch, the president will also be addressing the prosperity and security needs of the nation. While the president can chart the course for the nation, he will not be able to achieve it alone. The Air Force, as the dominant DOD player in space, has a significant role in advancing the nation's command of space.

Chapter 13

Wither Space in the USAF?

The Air Force is the house that aviators built on a proud theory of air power, even though, for most, the affection was really if truth be known, for the airplane. They wielded the theory as a sword to gain their independence and to claim primacy in military power ... But there were other dreamers abroad who looked to the stars.... The aviators, alas, instead of expanding their theory to the stars and extending the house to include its new domains, revealed by every decision their true affection, the airplane. ... the unity of the house slowly fractured; to be sure, the aviators continued to own the house, but no longer the loyalty of its occupants.[314]

Carl H. Builder
The Icarus Syndrome
1994

One of the foremost challenges facing the Air Force today is whether space operations will remain a part of the Air Force or whether it will eventually break off at some point in the future. Former Air Force Secretary Whit Peters and Air Force Chief of Staff, General Michael Ryan, both say the key to retaining the space mission lies in integrating space into Air Force operations. Significant progress toward this end has been made in recent months. In January 2001, General Ryan approved nearly all the recommendations put forth in the Commission to Assess United States National Security Space Management and Organization, also known as the space commission.[315] General Ryan foresees the day when a separate Space Force or Corps will be created but he sees it off in the future at least 50 years from now. However others, like General Ralph Eberhart, realize this is only the beginning and cautions that if the Air Force does not continue to further advance space, in terms of budget, space control, etc., over the next five years, the service will lose this mission.[316] This was indeed the subtle message conveyed by the space commission and the commission's chairman, Donald Rumsfeld, now Secretary of Defense is sure to be watching the Air Force's progress.[317] What is needed is a vision for the Air Force to command space, one that will ensure information dominance for national security and at the same time compliment the national vital interest of increasing economic prosperity.

To secure this national vision, the Air Force must transform itself from a space services provider into the guardian of the nation's space resources. To achieve this vision, the Air Force must go beyond the space commission's recommendations. If the Air Force can not reform, it is setting the nation up for a future Space Pearl Harbor. This transformation can begin with the following recommendations in these areas: organization, space doctrine, space ops culture, PME, funding/core competencies, and Space Force.

Organization

For any institution to successfully fulfill the "guardian of space" mission, the appropriate organizational structure must be in place. Currently, the Air Force is not structured for this role. It is noteworthy that the Air Force recently stood up a brand new space office on the Air Staff, XOS, to further integrate and advance space. While this is step in the right direction, there are further organization changes that are needed.

Information Operations

On 1 February 2001, Air Intelligence Agency (AIA) formally became apart of Air Combat Command. In general this is a good merger since it will "more closely mesh the Air Force's fighter, bomber and reconnaissance units with the people who collect and analyze information from satellite, aircraft, listening posts and other sources."[318] With this close association, there is the promise of better interaction between the operators and the intel personnel in planning and executing air operations. The end result is the Air Force is better organized to conduct its primary mission of flying and fighting. It is interesting to note that a similar merger occurred on the Air Staff, a few years ago, where intelligence was made a formal part (XOI) of the operations staff. The intended synergy for the full spectrum of operations is an admirable aim. However, there are parts within AIA that are better placed within Air Force Space Command.

Air Force Space Command is the Air Force's lead command for collecting and transmitting information. With this reality, it is only natural to see the synergy that would result from incorporating the information operations portions of AIA. More specifically, the 67th Info Ops Wing, 690th Info Ops Group, and the Information Warfare Center should all be merged with Air Force Space Command. With the acquisition of information operations capabilities, Air Force Space Command starts to build up the means to protect this information center of gravity in space. With arrows in their quiver, the space operators can also begin to develop the warrior ethos that the flyers rightly say is missing in the space community. This view is not to slight Air Combat Command's use of information but rather to point out that the amount of information "commanded" by Air Force Space Command is significantly greater. With this reality, it is only right that Air Force Space Command be given the Air Force lead for information operations and the requisite organizations to execute this responsibility.

In addition to building the tools to protect space, this merger would also facilitate terrestrial warfighting. U.S. Space Command is the sole unified command tasked with the responsibility for information operations. As currently structured, Air Force Space Command, Naval Space Command, and Army Space Command, all contribute resources to USCINCSPACE in time of crisis. If information operations remain in Air Combat Command, USCINCSPACE will potentially have to work with two Air Force four star generals, rather than one.[319] While this is not undoable, it certainly is not efficient. A better organization would allow USCINCSPACE to touch one four star general in the Air Force for any needed Air Force support. A minor point for consideration is the proposal by the space commission to create a new Under Secretary of Defense who is responsible for Space, Intelligence, and Information. The space commissioners saw the natural grouping of these related fields and so advocated for a single, high-level defense official responsible for these fields. While the Secretary of Defense organization certainly does not dictate what the organizational structure of the Air Force should be, the Air Force must be willing to adapt to those changes, which will provide the best security for this nation. An organizational change is also needed on the Air Staff.

Air and Space Tradeoffs

The newest Air Staff office on the operations side of the house is XOS, an office dedicated to integrating and advancing space within the Air Force. While the value of this office remains to be seen, another operations office, headed by the XO, should be stood up. Due to the volatility of this office's area of responsibility, this branch should be run by the XO directly. Currently there is no single Air Staff focal point where air and space tradeoffs are well thought-out and analyzed. With the triple realities of space technology rapidly advancing and offering new capabilities, many critical aircraft in a low density/high demand status, and a finite budget, it is more important than ever before that the Air Force thoroughly analyze the tradeoffs between space assets and aircraft. In addition, creation of this office would fulfill the DOD's 1999 space policy requirement for comparative assessments between space and terrestrial (air, sea, land) systems. While the policy implied this organization would be at the joint level vice Air Force or U.S. Space Command, the Air Force should still create this office.[320] The first reason is that the Space Commission recommended giving Title 10 authority to the Air Force as well as establishing the service as the DOD's executive agent for space.[321] With this empowerment, the Air Force needs to fully exercise this authority and thus conduct these tradeoffs. The second reason is that without these assessments, the Air Force is ill qualified to advocate the best, cost-effective approaches for expanding space.[322] The third and final reason is that if the Air Force does not step up to this responsibility, another organization will and the Air Force will have to live with the outside organization's recommendations. The Air Force should proactively determine its destiny in space to the maximum extent possible. When this office is stood up, it will immediately be in business since there are several assessments already waiting.

Two tradeoffs ready for analysis in the near term are the transition of the AWACS and JSTARS missions to space. As such, a number of questions should be addressed. What are the initial costs versus annual operations and maintenance costs? What are the total life cycle costs for space versus air? What is the transition timeline? Does technology or budget drive the transition? What stage of research and development is the technology that is needed to transition these and other missions to space? What option (space vs. air) will reduce personnel requirements? If the space option is chosen, will additional infrastructure need to be built? Another mission that should be studied for transition to space is ABCCC. If global awareness is possible from space, there is no reason why an aircraft must be in theater to perform this mission. Once the AWACS and JSTARS missions have transitioned to space, C2 of the battlefield could just as easily be performed from CONUS.

The recent Schreiver 2001 wargame, held in January 2001, demonstrated the effectiveness of a limited strike capability from space and thus highlighted another tradeoff for consideration. Imagine the ability to strike anywhere on the Earth, within two hours versus the 30 hours for a B-2. What are the costs for such a capability? What is the impact to the proposed F-22 and JSF acquisitions? Would this "strike from space" system impact the follow on to the B-52? What other missions are candidates for transition to space? All of these questions and more should be addressed in a single Air Staff operations office. Ideally this office would be a mix of air and space operators, acquisition experts, and engineers. Within the Air Force, this office would interact with SAF/AQ, air and space system program offices, as well as the NRO, Air Force Space Command and Air Combat Command. Outside of the Air Force, this office would interact with the other services, Joint Staff and SECDEF staff. Once approved, this office will prove to be immensely valuable in determining the right mix of air and space assets in the Air Force. However, the appropriate mix of assets alone is not enough to ensure dominance in space. The foundation for the proper employment of any weapon system begins with doctrine.

Space Doctrine

Perhaps the next most significant renovation needed in the Air Force lies in the area of space doctrine. Doctrine is an anthology of "best practices" based on experience. For the military, doctrine serves as the "Bible" for how to best conduct warfare. Doctrine for space operations is deficient for several reasons: lack of experience, lack of understanding, and lack of serious thought by the Air Force. Currently there is only one space doctrine document, AFDD 2-2, dedicated to Space Operations. Contrast this with the 2-1 Air Warfare series, which contains a total of nine documents.[323] Granted air power has been around much longer than space power but not nine times as long. The current AFDD 2-2 is written as a primer on space operations. It is not focused on what a space campaign is, how is it is planned, nor how it is integrated into air, land, and sea campaigns. The good news is that AFDD 2-2 is currently in revision and the draft has more of a warfighter perspective to it. Several of the chapter titles reflect this new focus: C2 of Space Operations, Space Superiority Ops, Global and Theater Space Ops, and Space Employment Concepts. However, even this rewrite is only scratching the surface.

This was readily apparent in the Schreiver 2001 wargame. There were many unanswered questions for which there was no doctrine. What are the limits for space control and space force application? What actions require National Command Authority approval? What are the options for countering the adversary's Intelligence, Surveillance, and Reconnaissance capabilities? What are the asymmetric strategies the adversary may employ? When is a preemptive "early deterrence strike" against a space ground station or an on-orbit asset the best strategy? When is it optimal to strike with a Common Aero Vehicle versus a manned bomber? What is the expected impact of information warfare attacks on the space infrastructure?[324] These and other questions only address one side of side of the equation—milspace issues. To only develop doctrine to address these issues would be myopic.

Air Force space doctrine must advance beyond the concept of space support or force enhancement for the services' combat forces. It must wrestle with the tough issue of force application or force projection in, from, and through space. The Space-Based Laser prototype will be on orbit is just over one decade. Now is the time to develop the doctrine that will guide the employment of this space weapon. Air Force doctrine must also address the impact of routine use of space—in, from, and through space. While we are not there today, we will certainly be approaching this threshold within the next five to ten years. Military issues are not the only important concerns to be addressed in Air Force space doctrine.

If the Air Force is to become the nation's true guardian for space, it must also address the commercial sector. This sector is woven into the very fabric and vitality of our civilian infrastructure and as such it must be protected. To not protect this source of wealth will directly impact the prosperity and security of this country. If doctrine is not in place for this mission, it will not occur or if it does, it will not be well thought out. The Schreiver 2001 exercise also exposed the need for doctrine in this area. Many questions remain as a result of actual space industry experts participating in the wargame. Who is responsible for warning commercial satellite owner/operators of impending attacks?

Who should provide protection for the commercial provider's terrestrial assets as well as on-orbit assets? How does the Air Force gain insight into the commercial providers' customers? If a customer is identified as supporting the adversary, what are the legal and contractual options to terminate this service? How do you attack a satellite system that is a consortium? How can the Air Force "surge" its space capabilities with commercial providers?[325] These and many more questions like these must be addressed by the Air Force if it intends to keep the space mission with in the Air Force. One explicit way to demonstrate the Air Force's commitment to the space mission is by developing the doctrine to address these issues. It must develop doctrine not only to establish space superiority but more importantly to command space.

Changing the Space Operations Culture

In the space commission's report, it was pointed out that the nourishment of the space culture within the Air Force has been neglected. Several recommendations were made to advance the space community's ability to execute our nation's space requirements. There are three additional areas where the space culture could be improved and strengthened: Air Force Specialty Codes, growing space experts and additions to the Developing Aerospace Leaders (DAL) program. These improvements also serve as incentives to recruit, retain, train, and invest in the AFSCs critical to building the nation's space infrastructure.

Air Force Specialty Codes (AFSCs)

Currently, the 13Sxx AFSC is the designator for the space and missile operations career field. In the past, these operations were two distinct career fields with their own

AFSCs. Due to the different cultures, which remain in each discipline and with good reason, the two fields should again be split out. This recommendation is clearly seen after an examination of each culture. In the Intercontinental Ballistic Missile world, many of the crewmember's options are taken away. No creative thinking is required or called for. It is a very checklist oriented environment, very "by the book." There are very good reasons for this regimented discipline. When personnel are entrusted with nuclear weapons, there can be no mistakes. With nuclear ops, each commander must be confident that every crewmember is operating exactly the same way—by the book. Thus, this discipline is exactly what is required for nuclear ops. This mindset or culture is in direct contrast with the space operations culture.

In the space arena, much more creative thinking is allowed while performing operations. This is to be expected since destroying a satellite, even if it is worth one billion dollars, pales in comparison to destroying a city or possibly starting World War III. The same analysis also holds true for the other disciplines within the space field. Perhaps the best illustration of this "creative thinking" is the formation of the Space Warfare Center (SWC) following DESERT STORM. A Blue Ribbon panel found that even though space was used like never before, it still was not understood or integrated to the extent necessary. The SWC's focus is on integrating space capabilities into the warfighter's weapon systems to maximize their effectiveness. More recently, the Space Battle Lab was created and co-located with the SWC. In a sense, this lab is the Air Force's equivalent of Defense Advance Research Projects Agency's (DARPA) Advanced Concept Technology Demonstration (ACTD) program, only the focus is on space related projects. Both the SWC and Space Battle Lab call for creative minds to advance and weave space into the warfighters' systems. Space Ops by its nature calls for this creative mindset.

Neither mindset, "by the book" or "creative," is better than the other is. To argue as such would be the equivalent of arguing whether the B-2 is better than the F-15. Neither is better and both are needed to successfully execute the air campaign. And yet, both have their own separate AFSC even though they are both engaged in air operations. Both the missile and space operators are engaged in space operations but both have different strengths. These strengths exist because there are different required cultures that reward accordingly. If one argues that these strengths could become even stronger by giving a person both experiences, then one need only look at the flying community again. Following this logic, an F-15 operator would be more effective if he is given a B-2 follow on assignment. While this scenario is certainly doable, to pursue it would be a waste of resources both in terms of dollars and human resources. A bomber operator is allowed to specialize in bomber operators while a fighter operator is allowed to specialize in fighter operations and together they participate in air operations with a net effect of the whole being greater than the sum of the parts.

Our nation's security demands experts in missile ops and space ops. By combining the two fields into one, we are creating a false illusion that we are creating professionals in both fields. This is not possible when the culture in each discipline is radically different. The mindset that is needed to succeed in the bomber community is different from what is required in the fighter community. Each respective culture is learned and strengthen as an operator is allow to remain is his own community. As a result, each community develops authorities on bomber and fighter operations. Once again, neither is better, they are only different and each is just as valuable. The space operations career field must look at and learn a lesson from the flying community's model for developing operator expertise.

If the space and missile career field is split, there will be those who say this action fosters "stovepiping" and continues a problem that the Air Force is attempting to rectify through the Developing Aerospace Leaders (DAL) program. If done without forethought, this is certainly true. Two methods for preventing this outcome are increased space Professional Military Education (PME) and vicarious experience in Exercises, Experiments, and Wargames (EEW). This method allows each group to be at least "schooled" if not experienced in the other AFSC. One way to formalize this education and training process is through an acquisition professional development program (APDP) like certification process.[326] Before advancing to the next level in the career field, one would complete mandatory professional requirements. Using this method prevents stovepiping within AFSPC and also aligns with DAL.

If we fail to take these steps, the nation will certainly have a host of space operators qualified in both missile and space operations but there will be very few experts. Therefore, when a crisis occurs, the human resources needed to effectively plan and integrate, missile and space operations into combat operations will be limited. When an air campaign is planned, a fighter operator is needed to answer fighter questions while a bomber operator is needed to answer bomber questions. For either to answer for the other would be talking out of school. Likewise, when a nuclear campaign is being planned, a career nuclear professional would be of most value as compared to someone with both space and missile experience. The same also holds true for space operations.

When planning a space campaign, a career space operator is of more value than someone who has both space and missile experience. To have both just dilutes the other. Separating the two career fields can strengthen each field.

If the Air Force chose to go down this road, it is inevitable that Air Force Space Command would highlight the real personnel issue of keeping the career field manned. Within the space community, the majority of operators go into missile operations rather reluctantly. In fact, many people are non-volunteered into missile ops. If the Air Force's goal is truly integration between space and air operations, many of the answers to the space community's questions can be found in the flying community. When pilots began to leave the cockpits in record numbers, the Air Force asked for and Congress approved the pilot bonus. The same could be done in the missile community—a missile operator bonus. The Air Force needs to clearly articulate this case before Congress and ask for the money. Who could argue with the reasoning that nuclear operations require career professionals? Yes, there is a cost to pay but it is small when compared with the confidence that is to be gained.

The 13Sxx career field as a whole stands to gain if space and missile operations both have their respective AFSCs and as a general rule, operators are allowed to remain within a single community. To aid with retention in missile operations, a missile operator bonus needs to be advocated for by the Air Force. If this recommendation is heeded and approved an addition change can further strengthen the competency of the space operators.

Growing Space Experts

If the space and missile career field was split, there would be five different types of space operations: space lift, space surveillance, early warning, command and control, and space control. The current wisdom given to junior space officers is to get at least three different operational assignments before you are up for major. The end result is a "jack of all trades, master of none." As a major, many of these officers then go on to the Air Staff or a MAJCOM. The problem with these operators is that their knowledge is a mile wide and an inch deep just when expertise in a subject matter is called for. This philosophy is self-defeating and is 180 degrees out of synch with the career progression advice given to the rest of the Air Force—"Depth then Breadth."

In the flying community, after initial flight training, the pilot is assigned to a primary aircraft. While this does not mean he cannot fly another kind of aircraft, it does mean that he will be a subject matter expert in that aircraft. Therefore, an F-16 pilot will typically have several F-16 assignments before going to Air Combat Command's staff or to the Air Staff. Imagine if the flying community followed the space model. A person could have an initial F-15 assignment followed by a B-52 tour and then one in a C-130. As a new major, he is now off to the Air Staff to work future fighter requirements. While this person is qualified, one F-15 assignment, he is certainly not the best qualified nor a subject matter expert. What is needed is a career expert in fighters, one who has been in the fighter cockpit for multiple assignments. The flying community model for growing pilot expertise should be adapted by the space community.

By allowing junior space operators to develop a core expertise first, "Depth," they are better prepared to take on a staff or other broadening assignments, "Breadth." Without this approach, a space operator can come to Air Force Space Command headquarters to work future space surveillance requirements with a career containing one surveillance assignment or maybe none. Wouldn't he be of more value with at least two surveillance assignments? To implement this model, one need only look to the flying community again. Upon graduation from initial space training, each individual would be assigned a primary weapon system. This would not preclude an individual from future assignments in other space disciplines, but he would remain an expert in the primary weapon system. As such, he can plan on at least two assignments in her primary weapon system before making major. When the time comes to be an Ops Officer or a Squadron Commander, Air Force Space Command would have a pool of experts from which to pick their key squadron leadership. In the flying community this is also true. In general, the squadron commander of an F-15 squadron is typically an F-15 operator just as the squadron commander of a B-52 squadron is most likely a B-52 operator.

The expertise within the space community can be raised if the above recommendation is followed. A direct result of this action would be operators who maximize their respective weapon systems. In this era of high ops tempo and increasing demands on existing weapon systems, the Air Force cannot afford to have operators who are not exploiting their systems to the fullest. Pursuing this course of action ultimately results in improved security for this nation. If these operators are subject matter experts, they will be better equipped to protect these weapon systems if threatened. One element of developing this space warrior ethos lies in the Developing Aerospace Leaders (DAL) program.

Developing Aerospace Leaders (DAL)

This recommendation in short suggests a way to introduce space operators into the flying community, more specifically the UAV community. It is recognized up front that this is a huge problem with an equally large gap in expertise for the space operator. A brief review of flying community makes this gap obvious: UAVs don't operate in space; they perform air missions (ISR, strike); space operators don't know and have not performed in planning or executing a Master Attack Plan, Air Tasking Order or air campaign yet UAVs would be part of these; and they have neither staff nor flying ops experience in much of what they would have to do. In addition to this training and education gap, this is a major culture change—allowing someone other than a pilot to fly a plane. Having stated this reality, if the Air Force truly seeks transformation of aerospace power, solving these problems comes with the effort.

DAL is an Air Force Chief of Staff initiative that is currently in work and the Chief plans to leave it as part of his legacy when he retires this summer. The premise of this program is that Air Force officers are too "stove piped" throughout their entire career and so when it comes time to be senior officers, they are ill equipped for the responsibilities at hand. For the space operator, the program recommends getting experience in space acquisition and information operations. While this certainly opens up the "broadening" opportunities, it is not open enough. Another opportunity that should be opened to space operators is Unmanned Aerial Vehicle (UAV) operations. There are several reasons for this recommendation.

The first is that space operators, as UAV drivers, would help with the current pilot shortage that is projected to remain with the Air Force for several more years. On top of this, most pilots are going to these UAV assignments rather reluctantly. The attitude of most space operators for flying UAVs is just the opposite; they would love to go. By filling all of the UAV flying assignments with space operators, more pilots are available for the cockpit. Another consideration is that using pilots to fly UAVs is not a wise management of the investment made in the pilots. The Air Force literally spends millions on each individual pilot so that he is able to fly some of the most sophisticated aircraft. A better investment would be to provide UAV training to the space operators. This investment certainly would not be in the millions of dollars and so the cost for training would be more in line with the cost of the UAV. A third reason is that this action would go a long way toward the goal of air and space integration. Currently pilots are allowed to integrate into space squadrons and even hold key positions up to and including squadron commander. In addition, pilots hold key staff positions at Air Force Space Command, NORAD and U.S. Space Command. If the Air Force is truly committed to integration, the reverse must also hold true; space operators must be allowed into the flying community. The easiest way to do this is to allow the space operators into the UAV squadrons. A fourth reason is that flying UAVs will get the space operators "in the fight" as well as help develop the "warrior ethos," both of which pilots say are lacking in the space community. Until space weapons are developed, this may be the closest space operators can get to actual combat operations. A final consideration is that most space operators already operate systems that are more complex and more costly than most UAVs. In fact, many space operators operate multi-hundred million dollar weapon systems that cost more than most aircraft. The space operators are ready; all they need is the training. This is a "win-win" recommendation for both the space operators and the pilots.

All of these recommendations, splitting 13Sx career field, growing of space experts, and flying of UAVs by space operators, help to maximize the human and equipment resources in the space career field. These resources can be further exploited by educating non-space officers about space. One institution that touches nearly every Air Force officer in an education capacity is Air University.

Professional Military Education (PME)

The Air Force's PME schools located at Maxwell AFB serve as the Mecca for airpower. In these schools, the awesome power of the air campaign is inculcated into the Air Force's finest officers. This is a good focus but it needs to be expanded. Currently, space is only thought of as a support function and the majority of instruction reflects this limited perspective. Instead, the focus needs to expand to look at space in the force application role. There were many lessons learned at the Schreiver 2001 space wargame, where force application from space was used, and one of them was to include key PME personnel in future wargames. Major General MacGhee, AWC/CC, participated in this year's wargame as the Joint Task Force Commander. To maximize the benefit of his experience, he is already making plans to include instruction on this new space role in next year's curriculum. The other school commandants at Aerospace Basic College (ABC), Squadron Officer School (SOS), Air Command and Staff College (ACSC), and School of Advanced Airpower Studies (SAAS), need to follow his lead and update next year's curriculum. There is a second initiative for the PME schools that will speed the integration of air and space operations.

The amount of space education taught at the Air Force's PME schools should increase and the level of instruction should be raised to match the level of the school.

Currently, there is not a "building block" approach for the space education taught at the various schools. A well thought out plan, which begins with the fundamentals of space in ABC and SOS, advances to the space campaign (operational level) at ACSC and culminates at the strategic level in SAAS and AWC, would greatly aid in raising the level of space education in the Air Force. While the Schreiver 2001 wargame will be incorporated into the AWC 2002 curriculum, the majority of the students will only profit marginally. This statement can be made because the majority of the students have had limited exposure to space in their assignments as well as limited education on this topic. This is evidenced by the Space Fundamentals elective that is taught at AWC. Two relevant facts stand out: 1) This is the highest demand elective, typically 20-30 students as compared to the average elective of about twelve students and 2) The level of instruction is at the basic level, it could easily be taught at ABC or SOS if so scheduled. Several conclusions are drawn from these facts: 1) Demand exceeds supply. Students are being turned away, even with the elective being offered twice in the year. 2) Students are taking this "basis" class because they have not had the opportunity previously in their career for this type of instruction nor will they likely have the opportunity later in their career. At AWC, space should be taught at the graduate level just like air operations are. For those who desire, there is a rigorous Joint Forces Air Component Commander elective. The same should be true for space but it must begin with space education in ABC. A third recommendation for PME schools concerns the commandants rather than the instruction or students.

During the past four commandants at Air Command and Staff College, the lead has alternated between a flyer and a space operator. The College's current commandant is

Brigadier select Sheridan who has experience as a space operator and in space acquisition. This is good trend, alternating the lead between air and space, but it need to be expanded to the other four PME schools, especially the School of Advance Airpower Studies. It would not be wise to have "all space" commandants or "all air" commandants at one time but rather about a 50/50 mix. While the space commandants have the lead, they must use their experience and contacts to bring space to their students. These schools ought to be on the cutting edge of defining what is a space campaign, what are the right weapon systems, what are the national policy implications, what are the international implications, etc. Integration is key to keeping the space mission and much of the space integration instruction can occur at the Air Force's PME schools.

Funding/Core Competencies

Perhaps the greatest challenge facing the Air Force in keeping the space mission is finding the dollars to fully develop this mission. Both former Secretary of the Air Force, Whit Peters and Air Force Chief of Staff, General Mike Ryan both have requested Title 10 authority for space but also petitioned for the corresponding dollars. In reviewing the Air Force's preparation for this year's Quadrennial Defense Review, one begins to appreciate the magnitude of the funding problem. Currently, the Air Force estimates a funding-resource mismatch of approximately 25 percent and this translates into an extra $20-30 billion a year. Out of this number, $10.2 billion is needed for air and space recapitalization.[327] Out of the $10.2 billion, $2.2 billion per year is needed to properly maintain the Air Force's space systems.[328] Although the services have already compiled their wish lists, Secretary of Defense Rumsfeld has put them on notice that the floodgates of money will not be opening.[329] With this harsh reality, the dollars for commanding space will not be found without innovative reform.

Before additional funds can be identified, for advancing space power, several assumptions must be made. First, the Air Force literally needs several billion dollars to truly advance the space mission. Two, the extra billions will not be found in the aircraft acquisition dollars. Three, the Air Force should not count on President Bush to provide the additional funds. Four, if President Bush raises the DOD's budget, a major portion of the space increase will go to the continued development of National Missile Defense, currently priced at $60 billion. Five, the Air Force must begin robust development of space control systems if it is to transform space from a support force to a warfighting force. If these assumptions are taken together, there is only one conclusion, the necessary funds must be found in the current space budget.

In this quest for additional funds, one must first review how the Air Force is providing space support to the Department of Defense. With approximately 90 percent of the services' budget and personnel for space, one is tempted to conclude that the Air Force is not lacking resources for space. However, the Air Force provides space services like a "utility company."[330] If you need space support, you contact the Air Force and sign up. Then when you need it, you turn it on and low and behold the Air Force space support is there. The major difference between the Air Force and a real utility company is that the Air Force is providing the space utilities at no cost to the customer. While a real utility company provides service to itself, it charges all other customers. To do otherwise would immediately bring financial ruin and the company would disappear. With this law of economics, it is admirable that the Air Force has been able to provide support, as long as it has, at no charge to the customer. The Air Force is facing a fiscal responsibility test with space dollars and as a result must reform immediately to pass the test.

If the Air Force is going to transform the space sector in five years, it should begin by charging the military services and other customers for space support. This "pay as you go" system needs to begin next year and be fully implemented within five years. This is not a new concept but rather one that was successfully implemented in the flying community. In the days of Military Airlift Command, the budgets were large enough to provide airlift free of charge. As the dollars for flying hours became tighter, this "free utility" policy was changed. Today, strategic or intertheater airlift, now provided by Air Mobility Command (AMC), is no longer free. It is a "fee for service" utility. With this new strategy, AMC is protected from going bankrupt in a flying year. The service is provided if the bill is paid. This same philosophy must be applied to the space community. The Air Force must propose a space "fee for service" system that provides the needed support on demand. While the other services will balk at this proposal, the Under Secretary of Defense for Space, Intelligence, and Information, a new position recommended by the space commission, can serve as the honest broker in negotiating the appropriate fees. This recommendation, while helpful, will not free up the billions needed for advancing space. As a result, more sweeping changes are required in the management of space. The Air Force must define its core warfighting competencies in space and then divest themselves of the excess space systems. It is just this kind of thinking that was highlighted in the Center for Strategic and Budgetary Assessment's

February 2001 "Quick Look" assessment of the DOD—divestment strategies are needed "to free up resources to support transformation."[331]

In choosing which space services to divest, the Air Force must face a challenging question, "What are the warfighting core competencies versus national utilities in space?"[332] One guideline to aid in answering this question is whether the space system is used solely by the military and national leadership or by a broader customer base. Once this question is answered, a second question immediately follows, "Who will be given responsibility for continued stewardship of this space utility?" It is only by answering these two questions that the divestiture analysis can begin. To motivate the Air Force to apply an aggressive divestment strategy, the service should be allowed to retain the budget for any divested systems. In this manner, significant resources can be generated, to advance the service's core space competencies, without raising the Air Force's total obligation authority. Currently, the military is dependent on space for the following utilities: weather/meteorological, navigation and timing, space surveillance, communication, spacelift, intelligence/surveillance/reconnaissance, early warning, space control, and nuclear weapons delivery. Each of these utilities must be scrubbed to determine if they are a warfighting core competency or not.

The Air Force started down this divestment path soon after DESERT STORM with the transfer of the Defense Meteorological Satellite Program (DMSP) to the National Oceanic and Atmospheric Administration (NOAA). With this transfer, all of the nation's meteorological satellite programs, military and civil, were combined into one organization. The true test of this new arrangement came when the military's requirement for weather information soared. In the Kosovo crisis, the weather support necessary was still available even though the military no longer owned and operated its own weather satellite. The DMSP transfer provides a successful template for analyzing whether additional space assets should be divested from the military.

Another space utility ready for transfer out of the military is the Global Positioning System (GPS). Although the military's use of GPS's navigation and timing information is increasing, it can be argued that the civilian use of GPS already exceeds that of the military. The growing dependence of the national and international sectors ensures this utility will endure for the military's use even upon transfer. Availability alone is not sufficient to met the changing requirements of the military. To guarantee the military's evolving requirements are met, the Under Secretary of the Air Force[333] would remain involved and influence the future design and direction of GPS. In the past, it was recommended that GPS be transferred to the Department of Transportation (DOT). The use of GPS has matured to the point where this utility is more of a national utility rather than an exclusive military utility and as such, the time is right to effect this transfer to DOT. GPS is not the only space utility that should be transferred to DOT.

Another space utility that should be split off from the military is space surveillance. Currently, the Air Force maintains a worldwide space surveillance system that benefits the military, civilian, and international communities. As the number of commercial launches continue to outpace the rate of military launches, this service is also evolving into a national utility. With this reality, the space surveillance system should also be transferred to the Department of Transportation. This is a natural transfer since the DOT already provides a national air utility service through the Federal Aviation Administration (FAA). It is a logical extension of the DOT to provide a civil FAA-like utility service for space. Divestment of this utility would include all of the Air Force's and Navy's space surveillance ground sites. To retain battlespace awareness of the space arena and maintain national security, the military would be defined as the DOT's most important customer. At times the military may want to conduct classified space surveillance operations—intelligence gathering missions, satellite engagements—and so the Air Force would continue to operate and task on-orbit space surveillance assets such as Mid-Course Space Experiment (MSX). As the review of military space utilities continues, the analysis becomes much more complex.

A fourth space utility for divestment consideration is satellite communication (SATCOM). Currently, this utility is the largest use of space both in and out of the military. With such competition in the commercial sector, one could reason that the military's SATCOM requirements should be completely outsourced. In time of conflict, this is already nearly the *modus operandi*. One has only to recall that in Kosovo, eighty percent of SATCOM traveled over commercial systems.[334] The commercial use of SATCOM must be balanced by the military's need for classified circuits. One method for fulfilling this requirement is with encryption units to encrypt and decrypt information passed through commercial systems. Before this recommendation is pursued, a detailed analysis is needed to determine if this approach is cost effective and at the same time satisfies the military requirements. If this approach proved to be the better way to conduct military ops, the Air Force and Navy SATCOM systems would be sold to commercial vendors. One SATCOM system that would remain under the Air Force's control is MILSTAR. This satellite system provides jam resistant communications in a nuclear environment and this capability is needed to ensure proper execution of the

Single Integrated Operations Plan (SIOP). The spacelift utility is also a candidate for commercialization due to the increased use by the business sector.

Spacelift is an even more complex utility service. On the one hand, commercial launches are the majority of business conducted at the spaceports each year but on the other hand the military and NASA have hard launch requirements each year. With the Air Force in control of the two major spaceports, national security launch requirements are more easily fulfilled when in conflict with commercial launches. In the past when the Air Force attempted to commercialize these launch facilities, the business sector balked at the offer. Perhaps one reason for this rejection is that the facilities are in dire need of modernization. In light of this reality, the Air Force is embarking on a twelve-year, billion-dollar upgrade to the launch facilities on the East and West Coast.[335] Another factor to consider is if the Air Force wants to get into the business of a "launch on demand" capability and eventually routine launch ops (e.g. single stage to orbit, Space Operations Vehicle), the Air Force may want to retain these assets rather than build new facilities. However, if these new systems do not require the huge infrastructure on either coast, perhaps the military is best served by divestiture of these spaceports and building new ones. There is no easy answer on who should own this utility service but as the number of commercial launches continue to dominate the launch manifest, it would appear the commercial industry should be given the responsibility. Further analysis is needed to properly weigh the U.S. government's interest in maintaining control of these facilities versus turning them over to commercial industry.

The space utilities that remain for divestiture analysis are intelligence/surveillance/reconnaissance (ISR), early warning, nuclear weapons delivery and space control. For each of these utilities, the virtually exclusive users are the military and national leadership. In addition, there is little growth of these utilities in the commercial sector with the exception of space imaging. The defining question is whether any of these utilities should also be divested from the Air Force. In the first category, ISR, all of these space assets are owned by the National Reconnaissance Office (NRO) and not by the Air Force. While the space imaging business is growing, transferring this utility to the commercial sector would not afford the required security for these "spy satellites." Rather than transfer these assets, the intelligence community should rely on the commercial sector to augment the classified collection when there is a surge in imaging requirements. These spy satellites provide a warfighting utility that should remain a core competency for the NRO. The same can be said for early warning, nuclear weapons delivery and space control. Since all of these utilities have a national security customer base with no growth in the commercial sector, they should form the basis for the Air Force's core warfighting competencies in space. It is on these utilities that the Air Force should concentrate and further invest.

The Air Force is already investing in the future of the early warning utility. The current constellation of Defense Support Program satellites will be replaced by the Space Based InfraRed System (SBIRS). To appreciate the magnitude of this commitment, one need only note that this program is the Air Force's largest space acquisition program. Likewise, the ICBM fleet is undergoing a multimillion-dollar modernization program to ensure the future of this utility. It is only in the last utility, space control, where commitment and budget is lacking.

Satellite Development

One area where space control should be advanced is in the development and operation of new on-orbit assets. Three candidates for consideration are dual-purpose satellites, serviceable satellites, and space surveillance satellites.

Perhaps the best example of dual-purpose satellites is the XSS micro-satellite series being developed at the Air Force's Research Laboratory: the XSS-10 Space-Based Proximity Operations satellite and the XSS-11 Space Ferry. Both of these micro-satellites are designed for a 24-hour on-orbit mission to service on-orbit satellites. The XSS-10 is a highly maneuverable satellite with high-resolution cameras, which allows for close proximity inspection. In theory, when the ground controllers notice a satellite is not functioning properly and the anomaly is not resolved from the ground, the XSS-10 is launched to investigate. The micro-satellite then maneuvers into close proximity of the malfunctioning satellite for an inspection. Based on the visual inspection, the ground controllers are better informed to resolve the anomaly. The XSS-11 is also a highly maneuverable satellite but designed with a different purpose—reposition satellites that did not achieve their operational orbits. Once an ailing satellite is identified, the XSS-11 satellite would mate with it and boost it into the correct orbit.[336] This is of great significance since many satellites can cost hundreds of millions and they cannot be fully exploited if they are not in the correct orbit. Due to their small size, both of these micro-satellites can be launched from a Pegasus or Taurus class booster. As such, this booster requirement allows a true "launch on demand" capability which is a "must have requirement" by the warfighter. This same micro-satellite, servicing technology could easily be turned into an offensive weapon against an adversary in space.

The responsibility for identifying all man-made objects in space falls to Air Force Space Command's Space Control Center (SCC) and NORAD's Combined Intelligence Center (CIC). However, there are times when these organizations fail to identify the payload on a new launch due to a lack of intelligence. If this happens in the future, the XSS-10 could be launched on demand and used in an intelligence-gathering role rather than a servicing role. With XSS-10 imagery, the SCC and CIC along with technical support from the National Air Intelligence Center, could assess in real-time whether a particular satellite was a threat or not. In time of crisis, this on-orbit inspection would be absolutely vital in assessing the space order of battle. Once an on-orbit threat is identified, the XSS-11 could be launched for the express purpose of repositioning the enemy satellite. Since many nations view satellites as "sovereign territory," repositioning of satellites is not something that could be done lightly—it would probably require National Command Authority (NCA) approval. However, the XSS-11 could have a variety of tactics, which would give a range of options to the NCA. The most severe tactic would involve mating with the target satellite and causing a deorbit or maximum repositioning boost. Another tactic not as severe would clip the satellite so as to shear off the command antenna or a solar panel. At the other end of the tactics spectrum, the XSS-11 could just bump the target satellite to destabilize it. Adding a small microwave or laser payload for "one-shot" stand off engagements could further enhance these tactics.[337] The Air Force should begin immediate operational testing of the XSS satellites both in a servicing and warfighting role. Once the concepts are validated, the satellites should transition from research and development into the acquisition world. The Air Force should then stockpile an inventory of these satellites and the necessary boosters for a launch on demand capability. With these resources on hand, the Air Force will be ready for future servicing missions as well as offensive engagements.

A second space control initiative requiring immediate attention is the fundamental design of all satellites. Currently the vast majority of satellites are not designed to be serviced on-orbit. One exception that proved the utility of a serviceable design is the Hubble Space Telescope.[338] Over the years, the Shuttle has periodically visited this billion-dollar satellite to replace an imaging lens, a solar panel and an electronic panel. This same concept must be further refined so satellites can be serviced on-orbit by XSS-type satellites.[339] Servicing should include but not limited to refueling and upgrading components. This concept would initially apply to low earth orbiting satellites and eventually expanded to higher orbits as breakthroughs in rocket propulsion are achieved. As with any program, it must remain cost effective to survive the annual budget reviews. As the concept of space engagements becomes a reality, the need for higher fidelity space surveillance increases.

To successfully employ support and offensive space tactics, the Air Force must first characterize the battlespace. For space engagements, this means access to accurate space surveillance information. One source of information would be the space surveillance network that was nationalize and turned over to the Department of Transportation. However, due to the highly politicized and international nature of offensive engagements, this source would probably not retain the secrecy warranted. For this reason, the Air Force should develop an on-orbit space surveillance capability to be used for just such engagements. This capability could consist of a three-ball Mid-Course Space Experiment (or similar type of satellite) constellation.[340] This scaled down space surveillance capability allows the space warfighter to have a dedicated system during all engagements. In addition, the cost for this system and the annual O&M is greatly reduced from the infrastructure of the global space surveillance network. This is a system tailored to meet the warfighter's battlespace awareness requirements. To be a true warfighter, one must have weapons. Once the warfighter is able to "Observe and Orient," he is then ready to "Decide and Act" or execute the mission. In other words, he is ready to engage with his weapons. This is another area in space where the Air Force should invest fiscal resources.

Space Weapons

One of the most controversial space issues facing the nation today is the weaponization of space. Currently, space treaties do not prevent this from occurring, with the exception of weapons of mass destruction (WMD). The 1967 Outer Space Treaty prevents the orbiting of WMD on orbit or the placement of such weapons on the Moon. In addition, military facilities can not be established on the Moon or other celestial bodies and weapons testing is not allowed.[341] Other than these restrictions, the U.S. is free to develop the needed resources to establish and maintain command of space. This is why the Space Based Laser (SBL) can be developed without violating the 1967 treaty. Even so, these weapon systems are highly political in nature. One has only to look at the SBL and NMD development to see that they will not go uncontested. Russia and China see these systems as destabilizing and possibly the start of a new arms race in space. Even so, these systems still need to be developed. This position rests on three realities—the first is that the U.S. has an enormous investment in space that continues to grow, second, space weapons have a long development cycle and third, the nation is currently limited in its ability to control space.

With the nation's growing reliance on space for communication, navigation and timing, reconnaissance, weather prediction, remote sensing, and a host of other disciplines, the U.S.'s investment in space continues to grow. Currently the U.S.'s investment is $100 billion and by 2010 the nation's investment is projected to grow to $500 billion.[342] In the next five years alone, it is estimated that $2 trillion will be pumped into the U.S. economy from the space business and related spin-offs.[343] The sheer magnitude of national wealth in and from space begs for protection of American space interests, much like the U.S. Navy of old protected maritime commerce. To protect the space infrastructure will require the development of space weapons.

The SBL illustrates the long, lead-time needed to develop an on-orbit weapon. This program began as a Defense Research Projects Agency program in 1977 and it was not until February 1999, that a contract was signed to design, develop and orbit the first SBL Integrated Flight Experiment (IFX) vehicle.[344] The IFX vehicle is not scheduled to go on-orbit until 2012 and the live fire demonstration to destroy a boosting missile is planned for 2013.[345] Even after this first launch, it will be several more years before the full complement of twenty SBLs are on orbit. It is during this time of strategic pause that these systems must be funded and developed. The nation must commit to development now while there is still time. If the U.S. fails to develop these weapons now, it will have limited options for responding to a future attack.

The third reality is that a nation can not protect its resources without some form of weaponry. Weapons are required since the vast majority of satellites are unprotected and thus, vulnerable to attack. In the marine environment this is called freedom of navigation while in the space arena this is called space control. Granted space control does not exclusively consist of space weapons but it is definitely a part of it. In the near term, the Air Force should begin fielding terrestrially based weapon systems with which to conduct offensive, combat operations. These systems would be a combination of fixed and mobile systems using either laser or directed energy to engage a target. Mobile systems allow for deployment into a crisis region and thereby afford the theater CINC an organic ability to better control the adversary's infosphere. These systems should be scalable to produce a wide range of effects: disrupt, deny, degrade or destroy. The reason for fielding these systems in the near term is that they are much more affordable, less technologically challenging and at the same time, more politically palatable. With these facts and the reality that terrestrial systems are already being employed around the world, the U.S. military must commit the needed resources to add these weapons to their arsenal.

Since the subject of on-orbit weapons is so emotionally charged in the international arena, the near-term focus for these types of weapons should be on research and development (R&D) rather than on fielding. The nation must maximize this time of strategic pause to break through the technological challenges of these complex weapon systems. If it fails to take advantage of this opportunity, the military is setting itself up for a future Space Pearl Harbor scenario. The current focus for on-orbit weapons should remain on R&D since it is a huge financial cost to make a system operational and the threat needs to become more apparent before the military can justify the cost. Today it appears the existing threats to space assets could be successfully contained with a combination of terrestrial lasers/directed energy weapons and conventional attacks on the adversary's space infrastructure. Once these terrestrial capabilities are exceeded, the on-orbit systems should then be fielded. While on-orbit weapons would certainly enhance the nation's ability to handle these threats today, the current threat does not warrant their fielding. A nature follow on subject to space weaponization is the creation of separate space force. If the space community possesses offensive weapons, should a separate Space Force or Corps be created?

Separate Space Force?

The Space Commission report underscored the need for the Air Force to better manage the space mission. In this admonishment was a warning that if it did not, the Air Force would loose the space mission in as little as five years. Senator Smith, who's legislation created the commission, praised this report and stated, "The Commission's recommendations lay the foundations for what I have often maintained—that we should evolve to the eventual creation of a separate Space Force."[346] Given these events, many in the Air Force are asking, "Should the space mission break off?" and if the answer is "Yes," the follow on question is "When and what would trigger this action?" It is not the purpose of this paper to advocate either position since events and lawmakers, rather than the military, will answer these questions. This is a political decision that will be driven by political circumstances and not necessarily some other logic. The events discussed above could drive the premature formation of a Space Force. Or, they could serve to preserve the space mission for an evolved Aerospace Force.

The creation of offensive space weapons, whether terrestrially or space based, is but one requirement for an effective space operations capability. In addition, launch operations and the related deployment of new space systems need to be a routine operation. To be effective and efficient they must not be planned months in advance but become a launch on demand operation as crises dictate. The third and final operational prerequisite is that these operations must be affordable. A look at the flying world is educational in illustrating these two points. One of airpower's greatest strengths is its ability to rapidly respond to any crisis, anywhere in the world. In addition to the inherent speed in airpower, a rapid response is possible because a sortie is a routine operation. A no-notice requirement can come down from higher headquarters in the morning and by the afternoon, the mission will be planned, briefed and ready for execution. This is only possible because the planning through execution of a sortie is a daily occurrence—it is a routine operation. When a crisis occurs, the airmen are ready since this is what they do on a daily business. The only thing that may be different in a crisis is the destination and the ordinance on board. The unstated reality in this flying example is that the airmen does not first check with the comptroller, to see if there are sufficient funds available, before executing his mission. The reason why one unplanned mission does not break the bank is because flight operations are affordable. If the mission, in response to a crisis, is of sufficient magnitude to bust the flying hours budget, the wing can appeal to Congress for a supplemental to cover the unplanned expense. All of these methods and practices need to be incorporated into space operations, particularly spacelift.

Currently spacelift operations are anything but routine. Launches are planned months if not years in advance. Satellites are then custom-assembled on the launch pad over a period of several months before the launch actually occurs.[347] This type of operation is anything but responsive to the needs of the military in time of crisis. What is needed is a launch on demand operation—launch when a crisis develops or when an unexpected failure occurs on orbit. To be "in the fight," a launch operation must be planned and executed before the crisis is over. If space is to become a major player in combat operations, this requirement for routine operations must first be fulfilled. Associated with this requirement is the need for affordable spacelift operations. A Titan IV launch can cost several hundred million dollars. Put another way, the cost to put one pound into low earth orbit is approximately $10,000 per pound.[348] With these types of operational costs, an organization is severely limited in the number of operations it can conduct. In addition, it could only afford few, if any, unplanned launches. A final factor is that Congress does not currently authorize supplementals for crisis operations in space. To be effective in space, launch costs must be significantly reduced to allow for routine, on demand operations. In addition to these three operational requirements for an effective space capability—offensive weapons, routine space operations and affordable operations—there are several other requirements, which were all previously mentioned.

In the space commission's report, the need for space senior leaders with a career in space was singled out.[349] These leaders provide for a "unity of command" that is based on experience and not rank. A space leader must lead space operations. This is not such a bold statement but rather a reality. Just look at the flying community. It is a given that air operations will only be lead by an airmen. The need for space general officers is even more critical if a Space Force is to be created. A related requirement is a space culture, which develops more expertise in all space officers. A second prerequisite is a space doctrine that lays out the best way to conduct offensive and support operations. The need for Air Force doctrine is readily apparent, but joint doctrine is also necessary. A recent GAO report highlighted this deficiency. It reported joint space doctrine has been in the works for ten years with no results. The logjam is due to disagreement by the services on the doctrine's content. With no joint space doctrine, all the services are ill prepared to fully utilized space assets in joint and coalition operations. A follow on effect is that the services' professional military schools are not equipped to build the appropriate curriculum to teach the employment of space forces.[350] The final requirement is adequate funding. Space operations are expensive by nature and look to remain so for the near future. With this reality, space can not advance without adequate funding.

All six of these requirements define the basis for an effective and distinctive space capability. Only time will tell whether the political decision-makers will use these criteria or another metric in resolving the space capabilities issue. Regardless, political leaders must be informed on the requirements for space capabilities whether they reside in an Aerospace Force or a separate Space Force so they can make decisions in the best interests of the nation.

One final note bears consideration. The Russian Armed Forces will soon have a new branch within their military—Russian Space Forces. This new branch has its origins in the Military Space Forces that were formed in 1992 and disbanded in 1997 when they were merged with the Strategic Missile Forces. Some Russian experts say this was a mistake which prevented the development of Russian Defense Ministry's capabilities in space.[351] The rationale for separating out a separate space force has a familiar ring; Senator Smith echoes this same sentiment.

Since the Air Force contains the majority of the nation's space resources—budget, personnel, and space assets—it must be prepared to shoulder the majority of the burden in taking the nation forward to command space. If it chooses not to step up to this responsibility, it risks loosing the space mission and perhaps slows the nation in its quest maximize the prosperity and security from space. However, even if the Air Force acts on each one of these recommendations, it alone will not bring about the vision of commanding space. Congress also plays an important role.

Notes

[252] Jennifer Palmer, "Air Force Pleased with Space Commission report," *Air Force Times*, February 5, 2001, 19.

[253] "Putin Says Russia Must Maintain Space Prowess," SpaceDaily, 3; on-line, Internet, January 31, 2001, available from http://www.spacedaily.com/news/russia-space-general-01e.html.

[254] *Webster's II New Riverside University Dictionary*, 1988 ed., s.v. "odyssey."

[255] "Chinese Space News," 2; on-line, Internet, December 18, 2000, available from http://www.geocities.com/CapeCanaveral/Launchpad/1921/news.htm.

[256] Major Jeff Witko and Major Jose Caussade, "GPS for Air and Space Power," February 12, 2001, No. 239.

[257] "Vietnam Working with Surrey to Build Microsats," 3; February 16, 2001, available from http://www.spacer.com/news/vietnam-01a.html.

[258] "Frequently Asked Questions," 4; on-line, Internet, February 8, 2001, available from http://164.214.2.59/general/faq.html.

[259] "NIMA Commission Report – Executive Summary and Key Judgments," 7, on-line, Internet, February 8, 2001, available from http://www.nimacommission.com/article02.htm.

[260] "NRO Commission Report: The Evolving Role of the NRO," 8, on-line, Internet, February 8, 2001, available from http://www.nrocommission.com/evolving.htm.

[261] "NRO Background," 2; on-line, Internet, February 8, 2001, available from http://www.nro.gov/background.html.

[262] "NRO Commission Report: Executive Summary," 2; on-line, Internet, February 8, 2001, available from http://www.nrocommission.com/exec_sum.htm.

[263] *Commission to Assess United States National Security Space Management and Organization, Executive Summary*, January 11, 2001, 2.

Notes

[264] William E. Burrows, *This New Ocean The Story of the First Space Age*, (New York: Random House, 1998), 329-330.

[265] Paul B. Stares, *The Militarization of Space*, (Ithaca: Cornell University Press, 1990), 18-19.

[266] Ibid, 19.

[267] Ibid, 47-48.

[268] Ibid, 49.

[269] Ibid., 51.

[270] Ibid. 51-52.

[271] The Discoverer name was used by the Air Force as a cover for the CIA's classified Corona program. Ibid. 44-46.

[272] Burrows, 306.

[273] Stares, 66-71.

[274] Ibid.

[275] Burrows, 320.

[276] On 12 April 1961 Yuri Gagarin was the first person launched into space. He was launched from the Baikonur Cosmodrome, which at the time was still in the Soviet Union. Today the Cosmodrome is located in Kazakhstan. Ibid, 321.

[277] Ibid, 321-322.

[278] Ibid, 323.

[279] Ibid, 329.

[280] Ibid, 428.

[281] Burrows, 535.

[282] The U.S. countered the Soviet co-orbital ASAT system with the F-15 launched Prototype Miniature Air Launched System (PMALS). Stares, 222.

[283] Burrows, 532-536.

[284] Burrows, 533.

[285] Stares, 217.

[286] Stares, 219.

[287] This program was later entitled Strategic Defense Initiative (SDI). Stares, 225.

[288] Burrows, 535.

[289] Stares, 225.

[290] The Congressional Budget Office says it will cost $60 billion over 15 years to protect the Nation from even a small number of ballistic missiles. "Missile Defense," April 26, 2000, 2; on-line, Internet, available from http:///www.fas.org/spp/starwars/program/news00/000426-nmd1.htm.

[291] Moscow and Beijing are leading the diplomatic charge against National Missile Defense (NMD). They are also seeking to exploit the European apprehension to further pressure President Bush to delay its deployment. Sergie Ivanov, secretary of the Russian Security Council warned the Bush administration that deployment of the NMD will trigger a new arms race that will extend into space. "Russia Steps up Campaign Against U.S. Missile Defense Plans," February 2, 2001, Agence France Presse, 2; on-line, Internet, February 2, 2001, available from http://www.russiatoday.com/news.php3?id=278483$section=default and Collen Barry,

Notes

"Russian Security Official Warn U.S. Against National Missile Defense," February 5, 2001, Associated Press, 3; on-line, Internet, February 13, 2001, available from http://www.space.com/news/russian_defense_warning_010205.html.

[292] "Escalating Space Race," 5 January 2001, 3; on-line, Internet, January 8, 2001, available from http://www.stratfor.com/home/giu/archive/S010701.asp.

[293] "Reusable Launch Vehicles (RLV's)," 4; on-line, Internet, April 4, 2001, available from http://www.stp.msfc.nasa.gov/rlv.html.

[294] Howell M. Estes, III, "The Aerospace Force on Today and Tomorrow, Transforming the Air Force Control the Vertical Dimension," in *Spacepower for a New Millennium, Space and U.S. National Security*, ed. Peter L. Hayes et al. (New York: MacGraw-Hill Companies, Inc, 2000), 173.

[295] The referenced wargames for 2000 were the Air Force's Global Engagement V and the Navy's Global 2000. In 1999's Global game, the Blue team elected to absorb Red's strike against U.S. space systems. However, for the rest of the game, the Blue team was severely hampered in its ability to handle Red's ballistic missiles since the allied early warning satellite system was damaged. William B. Scott, "Wargames Zero In On Knotty Milspace Issues," *Aviation Week & Space Technology*, January 29, 2001, 53-55 and William B. Scott, "Wargame: 'Space' Can Deter, Defuse Crises," *Aviation Week & Space Technology*, February 5, 2001, 40.

[296] General Estes quotes this percentage (15-20%) as the target amount such that the Air Force can properly execute nation security in space. Howell M. Estes, III, "The Aerospace Force on Today and Tomorrow, Transforming the Air Force Control the Vertical Dimension," in *Spacepower for a New Millennium, Space and U.S. National Security*, ed. Peter L. Hayes et al. (New York: MacGraw-Hill Companies, Inc, 2000), 173.

[297] "Chinese Press Blasts U.S. Space War Games," February 5, 2001, 2; on-line, Internet, February 13, 2001, available from http://www.space.com/news/spaceagencies/china_missile_defense_010205_wg.html and "Military Official Says China Should Prepare for Space Conflicts," February 13, 2001, 3; on-line, Internet, February 13, 2001, available from http://spacer.com/news/milspace-01g.html.

[298] Two space systems currently in development to which an offensive payload could be added is Mid-Course Space Experiment and Orbital Express. Both of these systems are discussed in the following section entitled, "Air Force: Integration or Separation."

[299] Quoted in Peter L. Hayes et al. "Spacepower for a New Millennium, Examining Current U.S. Capabilities and Policies," in *Spacepower for a New Millennium, Space and U.S. National Security*, ed. Peter L. Hayes et al. (New York: MacGraw-Hill Companies, Inc, 2000), 11. Other estimates call for at least 1,500 satellites to be launched internationally over the next decade. Either way, this is a vast marketplace for the U.S. to establish its economic dominance. "Escalating Space Race," 5 January 2001, 3; on-line, Internet, January 8, 2001, available from http://www.stratfor.com/home/giu/archive/010701.asp

Notes

[300] General Howell M. Estes, Commander in Chief, United States Space Command, address to Congressional Committee, Washington D.C., 1998, 17; on-line, Internet, 27 October 2000, available from http://sac.saic.com/space/docs/speeches/speech9.htm.

[301] Bruce L. Mahone, Director, Space Policy, Aerospace Industries Association of America, Testimony before U.S. House of Representatives Committee on Science Subcommittee on Space and Aeronautics, March 11, 1999, 3; on-line, Internet, January 19, 2001, available from http://www.aia-aerospace.org/aianews/testimony/tst_bm3_11_99.html.

[302] Frank Sietzen, Jr., "Spacelift Washington: The Future of Space: Part three: Commercial Space cooling trend continues," February 15, 2001, 2; on-line, Internet, February 16, 2001, available from http://www.spaceref.com/news/viewnews.html?id=287.

[303] Potential markets: 1) Power generation: The first source states that technology now exists to convert the sun,s energy at a rate of 42-56 percent. Most designs envision capturing the sun's solar energy via solar cells and then beaming the energy back to earth in the form of microwaves or laser beams, which are then converted to electricity. "A Constellation of Orbital Power," March 27, 2001, NASA Space Science and Simon P. Worden, "Space Control for the 21st Century, A Space "Navy" Protecting the Commercial Basis of America's Wealth," in *Spacepower for a New Millennium, Space and U.S. National Security*, ed. Peter L. Hayes et al. (New York: MacGraw-Hill Companies, Inc, 2000), 229-230, 2) Space Tourism: Japan and the U.S. are doing serious analyses on this new potential market. Aerospace Research and Development Policy Committee of the Institute of Electrical and Electronics Engineers—United States Activities, "What the United States Must do to Realize the Economic Promise of Space," December 17, 1993, 27; on-line, Internet, December 1, 2000, available from http://www.ieeeusa.org/documents/FORUM/LIBRARY/PAPERS/segrpt.html, 3) same reference as #2), 4) same reference as #2.

[304] "Reusable Launch Vehicles (RLV's)," 4; on-line, Internet, April 4, 2001, available from http://www.msfc.nasa.gov/rlv.html.

[305] The cancellation of these programs represented over a billion-dollar investment. The decision to terminate the X-33 and X-34 was made by NASA and not the White House—both programs were behind schedule and incurring too much technical risk. Leonard David, "NASA Shuts Down X-33, X-34 Programs," March 1, 2001, 4; on-line, Internet, April 4, 2001, available from http://www.space.com/missionlaunches/missions/x33_cancel_010301.html and "NASA cancels shuttle-replacement projects X-33 and X-34," March 2, 2001, 3; on-line, Internet, April 4, 2001, available from http://www.spacedaily.com/news/010302121444.kukn3guk.html.

[306] For more information on the X-34, please read the following reference. "NASA Takes Delivery of Boeing-Built X-40A," May 22, 2000, 3; on-line, Internet, April 4, 2001, available from http://www.spacedaily.com/news/rvl-00m.html.

[307] Dana Rohrabacher, Congressman, Chair of Space Subcommittee of the U.S. House Science Committee, "NASA's Space Launch Initiative Is Off Course," February

19, 2001, 3; on-line, Internet, April 4, 2001, available from http://www.aviationnow.com/content/publications/awst/20010219/avi_view.htm.

[308] Dana Rohrabacher, Congressman, Chair of Space Subcommittee of the U.S. House Science Committee, "NASA's Space Launch Initiative Is Off Course," February 19, 2001, 3; on-line, Internet, April 4, 2001, available from http://www.aviationnow.com/content/publications/awst/20010219/avi_view.htm and Stew Magnuson, "House to Hold Hearings on Space Launch Initiative Funding," February 14, 2001, 2; on-line, Internet, April 4, 2001, available from http://www.space.com/news/spaceagencies/rohrabacher_sli_hearings_010214.html.

[309] Steven Siceloff, "Goldin Likely Scapegoat as Congress Digs into NASA Budget," April 3, 2001, 3; on-line, Internet, April 4, 2001, available from http://www.space.com/news/spacestation/iss_congress_budget_010403.html.

[310] Siceloff.

[311] Space Frontier Foundation, "Space Frontier Foundation Says: 'Space Launch Initiative Program (SLIP): Fix it or Kill it,' February 8, 2001, 2; on-line, Internet, April 4, 2001, available from http://www.spaceref.com/news/viewpr.html?pid=3787.

[312] "Cheap Access to Space A Policy for the 21st Century," 2; on-line, Internet, January 19, 2001, available from http://www.space-frontier.org/POLICIES/cats-policy.html.

[313] Jerry Grey, Director, Aerospace and Science Policy, American Institute of Aeronautics and Astronatics, "Barriers to Commercial Space Launch," Statement to Subcommittee on Space and Aeronautics Committee on Space, U.S. House of Representatives, June 10, 1999, 5; on-line, Internet, January 19, 2001, available from http://www.house.gov/science/grey_061099.htm.

[314] Carl H. Builder, *The Icarus Syndrome*, (New Brunswick: Transaction Publishers, 1994), xxii.

[315] Lt. General "Doc" Foglesong, "Space Commission Implementation (SCI) TF" briefing, Jan 2001.

[316] "Ryan Says Space Force Unwarranted For Next Fifty Years," *Aerospace Daily*, February 9, 2001.

[317] William B. Scott, "USAF Warned To Bolster Or Lose 'Space Force' Franchise," *Aviation Week & Space Technology*, January 29, 2001, 55.

[318] Bruce Rolfsen, "Intelligence agency to merge with Air Combat Command," *Air Force Times*, February 19, 2001, 11.

[319] This scenario seems likely as a result of the space commission's recommendations. It appears Air Force Space Command will have a new four star commander who is not also dual hatted as the commander of U.S. Space Command. Air Combat Command already has a four star commander.

[320] General Accounting Office, *Defense Acquisitions: Improvements Needed in Military Space Systems' Planning and Education*, May 18, 2000, Report Number NSIAD-00-81, 6.

[321] *Commission to Assess United States National Security Space Management and Organization*, January 11, 2001, 89.

Notes

[322] General Accounting Office, *Defense Acquisitions: Improvements Needed in Military Space Systems' Planning and Education*, May 18, 2000. Report Number NSIAD-00-81, 6.

[323] "Air Force Doctrine Documents," 2; on-line, Internet, February 23, 2001, available from http://www.doctrine.af.mil/Library/hierarchy.asp.

[324] William B. Scott, "Wargames Zero In On Knotty Milspace Issues," *Aviation Week & Space Technology*, January 29, 2001, 52-55 and William B. Scott, "Wargame: 'Space' Can Deter, Defuse Crises," *Aviation Week & Space Technology*, February 5, 2001, 40-41.

[325] Scott, "Wargame: 'Space' Can Deter, Defuse Crises."

[326] General Mitchell discussed his idea of an APDP-like (acquisition professional development program) program for the space field as an alternative to a Space Force or Corps. Just as there are requirements to advance professionally in the acquisition career field, there could also be professional requirements to advance in the space and missile career field. Major General Howard Mitchell, AFSPC/DO, informal discussion with AWC space operators on the Space Commission results, Air War College, Maxwell ARB, AL, 27 March 2001.

[327] Jennifer Palmer, "Respect and money, We deserve more of both, Air Force says in new QDR," *Air Force Times*, February 12, 2001, 8.

[328] Stew Magnuson, "Air Force Claims It Needs $2.2 Billion More a Year for Space Assets," January 12, 2001, 2; on-line, Internet, Jaunary 17, 2001 available from http://www.space.com/news/spaceagencies/air_force_space_funding_010112.html.

[329] Thomas E. Ricks, "Pentagon Study May Bring Big Shake-Up," *Washington Post*, February 9, 2001, Page A01.

[330] The germ of the idea of the Air Force providing space support as a utility company came about in discussions with Lt. Col. Dave Ziegler. Lt. Col. Dave Ziegler, 76 SOPS/CC, Peterson AFB, CO, interviewed by author, 27 January 2001. Lt. Col. Ziegler in turn gave credit to Lt. Col. Cynthia A. S. McKinley for the space utility analogy. Lt Col Cynthia A. S. McKinley, "The Guardians of Space: Organizing America's Space Assets for the Twenty-First Century," *Aerospace Power Journal*, Spring 2000.

[331] "A Strategy for a Long Peace," briefing, Center for Strategic and Budgetary Assessments, February 12, 2001.

[332] This same question is addressed in Lt. Col Cynthia A. S. McKinley's "The Guardians of Space" paper but with a different conclusion. She proposes a equally thought provoking solution with the creation of a Space Guard, similar to the Coast Guard, that is responsible for providing space utility services. In time of peace, the Space Guard would report to the Department of Transportation and in time of crisis, report to the U.S. Air Force.

[333] In the space commission's report, it is recommended the Under Secretary of the Air Force serve as the single Acquisition Executive for Space—both black and white space. With this consolidation of responsibilities, there is one focal point to ensure the needs of the military are met with the on-going and future space acquisitions. It is in this role that the Under Secretary would remain involved and influence the future capabilities of GPS.

Notes

[334] Peter Grier, "The Investment on Space," February 2000, 8; on-line, Internet, October 27, 2000, available from http://www.afa.org/magazine/0200investment.html.

[335] Daniel Sorid, "Launch Range Upgrades Nearly Complete," September 3, 1999, 2; on-line, Internet, March 26, 2001, available from http://www.space.com/missionlaunches/launches/rsal_over.html.

[336] "Kirtland MicroSat toFly 2000," July 23, 1998, 3; on-line, Internet, April 2, 2001, available from http://www.spacedaily.com/news/microsat-98e.html and "XSS Micro-satellite," 2; on-line, Internet, April 2, 2001, available from http://www.boeing.com/defense-space/space/xss and "XSS-10," 2; on-line, Internet, April 2, 2001, available from http://www.te.plk.af.mil/teo/missions/xss10/xss10.html and Briefing, Air Force Research Laboratory Space Vehicles Directorate, Kirtland AFB, NM, subject: XSS microsatellites, September 2000.

[337] There are numerous ways to blind or "dazzle" a remote sensing satellite or to interfere with a communication satellite. A laser on the ground or in space could dazzle a satellite's optical components—imaging optics, star sensors, and horizon sensors. Another method of interference is to jam the space-ground link. High-power microwaves can disrupt, degrade and destroy satellite electronics. Theresa Foley, "Space: 20 Years Out," February 2000, Air Force Magazine, 7; on-line, Internet, November 30, 2000, available from http://www.afa.org/magazine/0200space.html.

[338] The Hubble Space Telescope was designed to be visited about every two years for repair missions. Hubble has been visited three times for repair, 1993, 1997, 1999 and a fourth mission is scheduled for November 2001. Steven Siceloff, "Columbia to fly repair mission to Hubble," *Florida Today*, April 2, 2001; on-line, Internet, April 3, 2001, available from http://www.flatoday.com/news/space/stories/2001a/apr/spa040201a.htm.

[339] A similar on-orbiting servicing satellite is also being developed by Defense Advanced Research Projects Agency (DARPA). The Orbital Express satellite is designed to "demonstrate robotic techniques for on-orbit preplanned electronics upgrade, refueling, and reconfiguration of satellites." This satellite will support future U.S. national security and commercial satellites. The first demonstration satellite is scheduled for launch in 2004. "Orbital Express Space Operations Architecture/ASTRO," March 21, 2001, 2; on-line, Internet, April 2, 2001, available from http://www.darpa/mil/tto/PROGRAMS/astro.html.

[340] The requirement for a "three-ball" constellation versus any other size constellation came from discussions with Lt. Col. Bryant Anderson on the subject. Lt. Col. Anderson's squadron is the command and control node for the global space surveillance network. Addition MSX spares would need to be in the "barn" to allow for rapid replacement or to surge to a larger constellation in time of crisis. If national missile defense is also dependent on this system, the constellation size would need to expand accordingly. Lt. Col. Bryant Anderson, 1st Space Control Squadron/CC, Cheyenne Mountain AFB, CO, interviewed by author, 29 March 2001.

[341] *Treaty on Principles Governing the Activities of States in the Exploration and Use of Outer Space, Including the Moon and Other Celestial Bodies*, US ratification at Washington, London, and Moscow on October 10, 1967.

Notes

[342] "Escalating Space Race," 5 January 2001, 3; on-line, Internet, January 8, 2001, available from http://www.stratfor.com/home/giu/archive/010701.asp and Richard J. Newman, "The new space race," U.S. News and World Report, November 8, 1999, 7; on-line, Internet, November 13, 2000, available from http://www.usnews.com/usnews/issue/991108/space.htm.

[343] General Howell M. Estes, Commander in Chief, United States Space Command, address to Congressional Committee, Washington D.C., 1998, 17; on-line, Internet, 27 October 2000, available from http://sac.saic.com/space/docs/speeches/speech9.htm.

[344] United States Air Force, "Fact Sheet—Space Based Laser Integrated Flight Experiment," 2; on-line, Internet, March 29, 2001, available from http://www.sbl.losangeles.af.mil/Divisions/FrontOffice/sblifx_fsheet.htm.

[345] 'Space-Based Laser Team Define Requirements for Experimental Missile Defense System," April 4, 2001, 3; on-line, Internet, available from http://www.spacer.com.news/laser-01d.html.

[346] Senator Bob Smith, "Smith Issues Preliminary Comments on Space Commission Report," January 11, 2001, 2; on-line, Internet, February 13, 2001, available from http://www.senate.gov/~smith/Releases/Releases/01112001a.HTM.

[347] John T. Cornell, "Fogbound in Space," Air Force Magazine, January 1994.

[348] "Reusable Launch Vehicles (RLV's)," 4; on-line, Internet, April 4, 2001, available from http://www.stp.msfc.nasa.gov/rlv.html.

[349] Commission to Assess United States National Security Space Management and Organization, January 11, 2001, 42-44.

[350] General Accounting Office, Defense Acquisitions: Improvements Needed in Military Space Systems' Planning and Education, May 18, 2000, Report Number NSIAD-00-81, 8-9.

[351] The command structures and strategies for this new service are being put together for a June 1st activation. "Russian Space Forces To Be Formed by June 1st," April 4, 2001, 3; on-line, Internet, available from http://www.spacer.com/news/russia-military-general-01b.html.

Chapter 14

Making the Investment

In 1491, the year before Christopher Columbus landed near North America, doing business in India and China was probably as difficult as doing business in space is now. It was easily as expensive, and certainly more risky. But doing business in India or China today is routine. The cost and safety risks have been dramatically reduced. Thus, if the economics are right, the trip will be seen as worthwhile. The same logic can apply to space. Government policies should encourage, and not hinder, creative private sector plans for making space just another place to do business.[352]

Keith Cahoun-Senghor
Director, Office of Air and Space Commercialization
1996

One of Congress' most powerful responsibilities is the power of the purse. Within the U.S. government, they embody the "golden rule"—"He who has the gold, rules." For the nation to pursue any national objective requires the support of Congress to authorize and appropriate the necessary funds. Without this support, the quest, while a worthy one, will flounder in its creation. The quest to command space is certainly no different. With the high cost of space and the current interest in space, Congress has a definite and important role to play in three major areas: funding for space, monitoring of space transportation development and creation of a commercial space surge capability.

Space Funding

To begin the quest to command space, Congress in consultation with the military must determine the appropriate funding level for space, whether it remains in the Air Force or becomes a separate Space Force. One proposal, which needs congressional review, is the one presented earlier in this paper. This proposal divested space utilities that are becoming more national versus military in nature. Furthermore, this proposal recommended the Air Force keep the budget associated with these divested programs. These funds would in turn be used to develop new space control systems. In this manner, the Air Force's total obligation authority remains the same and at the same time the money allocated to space is better focused on the security needs of the nation. The departments receiving the divested programs would need an associated plus up in their budget. The initial years of this divestiture would be costly due to the construction of new space infrastructure faculties. Subsequent years would be more manageable with only acquisition and operations and maintenance costs.

If Congress rejects this proposal, another alternative is to keep the military space programs in their respective services. If Senator Smith and others in Congress are truly committed to developing space control systems, the Air Force will need a "plus up" in their budget. In the past, Senator Smith accused the Air Force of advancing the flying community at the expense of space. To correct this perception, the Space Commission recommended the creation of a major force program (MFP) for space.[353] This action would in effect "fence" space monies so they could only be used on space programs. On initial thought, this appears to be a good way to manage the space budget. However, there is a downside. Since the money is fenced, it is just as difficult to put additional Air

Force monies into this pot of money as it is to take money out of it. Perhaps all that is needed is better insight into how the Air Force spends the space funds appropriated by Congress. If Secretary of Defense Rumsfeld recommends against a MPF in his testimony to Congress,[354] an alternate accounting system would be an annual report to Congress on the DOD's expenditure of space dollars. The Air Force will have a vested interest in this report since this will demonstrate their fiscal stewardship of the space appropriations.

Congress can assist the nation in appropriating the funds necessary to advance space control. While the amount of additional funds is currently undefined, Congress should hold hearings with the SECDEF and SECAF to flush out this number as well as define what is the best organizational structure for the military's current space systems. If the decision is made to divest some of the Air Force's space programs, Congress will need to appropriate the necessary funds for these additions. If done in a timely manner, this increase could be added to the 2002 DOD Appropriations bill. A second space issue that requires the attention of Congress is the advancement of space transportation. While the president can take the lead on this issue, Congress's "power of the purse" is needed as well as its oversight role.

Monitoring Space Transportation Development

The need for President Bush to take the lead in calling for and supporting a national objective of reducing the expense of spacelift was mentioned earlier. With the cost of launch at $10,000 per pound, this is the greatest technological challenge facing the advancement of space. If the U.S. is able to take the lead in reducing launch costs one order of magnitude and eventually a second order of magnitude, it will be well on its way to commanding space. With this breakthrough comes increased prosperity and security, as new marketplaces are opened and new capabilities are deployed on-orbit. However, there will be great developmental costs along the way to achieving this ambition, much like the European nations of old opening the trade routes to the East. These costs cannot be bore by the commercial sector alone. The U.S. government must step in and take the lead since this technological breakthrough is in the vital interests of this nation, not just the commercial sector. A recent example of this support by the government is the development of the newest class of heavy lift boosters—Evolved Expendable Launch Vehicle (EELV). The government gave $500 million each to Lockheed-Martin and Boeing to aid in this development.[355] Another example, discussed earlier, is NASA's Space Launch Initiative for advancing Reusable Launch Vehicles. These initiatives are both steps in the right direction but they are evolutionary rather than revolution in nature. It is this kind of financial support that the Congress must continue since true command of space all begins with this first accomplishment.

To heed the President's call, for a national commitment to greatly reduce the cost of launch, will require a long-term fiscal commitment that will extend over a decade. The race to the Moon never would have been won if partisan politics had prevailed or if the support ended after one administration. Before the money is authorized and appropriated, Congress should appoint another commission to focus on this single issue. This legislation should be put into the FY2002 budget appropriations bill with the commission's first meeting in January 2002. The commission's report should be out in six months to allow for new legislation to be put into the FY2003 budget. The scope of the study should include issues such as: What is the national strategy to first reduce the cost of launch one order of magnitude and subsequently an additional order of magnitude for both ELVs and RLVs? Who will have the lead for this technological challenge? What is the role of NASA, DARPA, the DOD and the aerospace industry in this quest? How will these organizations interact and coordinate with each other? How much financial assist should be given to each ELV and RLV participant by the U.S. government? What are the milestone completion criteria that will allow continued funding from year to year? Until these questions are answered, Congress is ill equipped to provide additional funds. Once this strategic plan is in place, both the DOD and NASA should report to Congress, at least once a year, the progress made to date. Keeping Congress involved in this costly venture has two benefits: 1) it allows them to remain cognizant of the developmental progress and how the nation's wealth is being used and 2) over time they develop a stake in this quest and hopefully their future support is won. America's prosperity and security can be certainly advanced in the 21st century if Congress is willing to commit to a long-term investment for space transportation. Without this support, the nation will proceed much slower and continue to lose marketshare. This in turn will erode America's well being. There is another space issue in which Congress can further the prosperity and security of the nation.

Creation of Commercial Space Surge Capability

The National Space Policy seeks to stimulate private invest in the commercial space sector by committing the U.S. Government to buy commercially available goods and services.[356] With the explosion in the commercial satellite communication and remote sensing business, the time is right for the DOD to consider supplementing their current space capabilities with commercially available services. The precedent has already been set for this type of cooperation between the military and the commercial sector with the success of the Civil Reserve Air Fleet (CRAF). While CRAF is used in a nominal way in time of peace, its true value is seen in time of crisis. Even though it took six months to get ready for DESERT STORM, the activation of CRAF to Level II prevented it from taking even longer. The same case can be made for communication and remote sensing satellites.

The most recent major military engagement in Kosovo reminded the military that space assets are Low Density/High Demand (LD/HD) resources. For satellite communications, it was earlier discussed that eighty percent flowed through commercial satellites. In addition, the military's communication requirements continued to grow at a phenomenal rate. Consider the aforementioned fact that the amount of bandwidth required for ALLIED FORCE was five times the amount required for DESERT STORM. This harsh reality supports the need for a Commercial SATCOM Reserve Fleet. For the imagery side of the house, it is unknown what the actual requirements versus supply were since much of the imagery is collected by the National Reconnaissance Office (NRO) and is thus classified. However, Mr. Hall, Director of the NRO, talked about the LD/HD nature of imagery satellites over Kosovo.

> What we have found in our imagery architecture and one of the main things of [Future Imagery Architecture] is not how many pictures you can take in a day, but how many pictures can you take over Kosovo in a day. It is a lot less what you can take over Kosovo than what you can take over the world. And in those type of situations, I would anticipate that a combination of airborne, commercial, and FIA in a region like Kosovo or North Korea or something like that, we still will be stressed to get all the information to support what people can properly use to make wise decisions.[357]

Mr. Hall's comments support the formation of a Commercial Imaging Reserve Fleet. Both of these initiatives leverage the DOD's precious space dollars and at the same time expands the nation's prosperity and security. While the details of how these programs could be implemented is beyond the scope of this paper, Congress in concert with the DOD should take a serious look at creating these programs. Major Douglas Rider and others have written about the need for a Commercial Imaging Reserve Fleet but little work has been done for the equally necessary, Commercial SATCOM Reserve Fleet.[358] In addition to considering the needs of the U.S. military, Congress must also take into account the needs of NASA and the U.S. Geological Survey (USGS), who are the other primary users of imagery in the government. Given the national scope of this initiative, Congress should task the DOD, NASA and USGS to deliver a coordinated plan to Congress. If this fails, Congress could appoint another six-month commission to formulate a harmonized plan for all the needs of the government. The same type of tasking should be given to the DOD to develop a service-coordinated plan for the use of commercial SATCOMs.

The continued involvement of Congress in the quest to command space will only strengthen the nation's resolve toward this goal. By advancing space, prosperity and security is advanced and thus the well being of the nation is improved. As Congress remains a vital part in the advancement of space, they are better able to articulate the derived benefits to their constituents and thus better able to take the long-term view in supporting space advancement with the power of the purse.

Notes

[352] Keith Cahoun-Senghor, Director, Office of Air & Space Commercialization, U.S. Department of Commerce, "Trends in Commercial Space 1996," 2; on-line, Internet, 13 October 2000, available from http://www.ta.doc.gov/space/tics/intro-text.htm.
[353] Ibid., 76, 96-97.
[354] SECDEF Rumsfeld will present the DOD's implementation plan on the Space Commission's recommendations to Congress on 12 April 2001. Lt. General "Doc" Foglesong, "Space Commission Implementation (SCI) TF" briefing, Jan 2001.

Notes

[355] The EELV program's goal is to reduce the cost of access to space by 25 percent. In October 1998, the Air Force awarded contracts to Boeing and Lockheed Martin. Both contractors received a $500 million development contract as well as a contract to build the boosters. Lockheed Martin was award a $1.15 billion contract for nine launches of its Atlas-derived booster and Boeing was awarded a $1.38 billion contract for 19 launches on its Delta IV booster. "EELV Evolved Expendable Launch Vehicle," 12; on-line, Internet, April 6, 2001, available from http://www.fas.org/spp/military/program/launch/eelv.htm and "Air Force Announces EELV Contracts," October 17, 1998, 2; on-line, Internet, April 6, 2001, available from http://www.spaceviews.com/1998/10/17a.html.

[356] Marc J. Berkowitz, "National Space Policy and National Defense," in *Spacepower for a New Millennium, Space and U.S. National Security*, ed. Peter L. Hayes et al. (New York: MacGraw-Hill Companies, Inc, 2000), 41.

[357] Major Douglas B. Rider, "Establishing a Commercial Reserve Imagery Fleet: Obtaining Surge Imagery Capacity from Commercial Remote Sensing Satellite Systems during Crisis," in *Chairman of the Joint Chiefs of Staff Strategy Essay Competition, Essays 2000*, (Washington D.C.: National Defense University Press, 2000), 54.

[358] In his research, Major Rider mentioned three other independent sources for the CRIF concept. 1) Commercial Imagery Program, National Imagery and Mapping Agency, *Frequently Asked Question, NIMA Use of Commercial Imagery* (October 15, 1999). 2) Chris Allen, "Civil Reserve Imaging Fleet Proposal," Proposal viewgraph slides (Bethesda, MD: NIMA/PAS). 3) Institute for National Security Studies, "Space Policy—Topic 14, Propose New Business Practices Whereby the U.S. Military Can Obtain Needed Surge Capacity on Commercial Systems During Times of Crisis," Air University Research Topics, August 9, 1999, on-line, Internet, 6 October 1999, available from http://research.maxwell.af.mil/Topics_Database/display_topic.asp?topicNbr=326. Major Douglas B. Rider, 47-73.

Chapter 15

Conclusion

There is one thing stronger than all the armies of the world, and that is an idea whose time has come.[359]

Victor Hugo

Space is an indispensable part of American society. From entertainment to safety, from business to scientific research, space is there whether Americans know it or not. The knowledge gained from space enables a comparative advantage in the international arena, both in the business sector and the military. This in turn serves to preserve and promote the nation's prosperity. As the U.S. national quest for knowledge and wealth continues, it is sure to repeat the economic development cycle experienced by the Europeans in their quest to command the sea. Their quest was motivated by the desire to promote the national well being of their countries and expand their share of the maritime marketplace. This timeless cycle is Exploration, Knowledge, Exploitation, Investment, Consumption, and Protection. Early space visionaries focused on the exploration and knowledge phases of this cycle. One could say space had its greatest manifestation of these stages with the landing on the Moon. The pursuit of these two continue but they do not capture the attention of the American public. The focus in space is now on exploiting this market for investment and consumption. The rise and fall of a nation can many times be traced to a lack of protection for its source of national wealth. The historical experience of European nations and their naval competition are but one example of this truth. The same will happen to this nation if we fail to protect our wealth in space. Space is a vital national interest that is currently a strategic vulnerability rather than an unchallenged source of security.

Space assets today are an Achilles' heel. They represent a strategic military and commercial vulnerability. This vulnerability presents an easy target for an asymmetric attack against this nation. Not only would the military suffer but so would the well being of the entire nation. Until this nation develops the means to protect space and what it provides, it places both its prosperity and security at risk.

The time has come for this nation to pursue boldly the vision of commanding space. This vision is not a quest that can be accomplished by any one person or organization. It will require a long-term commitment of the government, the commercial sector and the American public. Even so, the military must stand up and answer the call for the protection of our nation's space sector. The U.S. Navy has successfully protected maritime commerce for over two hundred. The Air Force, as the principle custodian of the third dimension—air and space—must step up to the challenge of protecting our nation's space infrastructure. The time is right—fiscally, politically, and strategically— and the Air Force can not afford to miss this opportunity. If it does, it risks losing the responsibility for being not only the nation's guardian of space, but also a major source of its security.

The first step is the statement of the vision, which this paper attempts to do. The next step in this vision to command space is education—of the military services, the American public, and the politicians. Without an understanding of the importance of space, none of these groups will give their long-term commitment to achieving this goal. This must be followed with a willingness of government to foster cooperation with and assistance to the commercial sector to maintain current markets in space as well as develop new ones. Finally, the military must expand its capabilities to include the protection of the nation's assets and interests in space. But a failure to embrace this vision to command space places the prosperity and security of the nation at risk.

ENDNOTES

Notes

[359] QuoteGallery.com, search by key word: "idea whose time," 2000, 1; on-line, Internet, April 3, 2001, available from http://www.quotegallery.com/asp/search.asp.